# Transformation After Trauma

## Embracing Post-Traumatic Growth

# Stephanie M. Hutchins, PhD

# Dedication

*To those that feel, or have felt,*
*that the darkness will never end.*

# Table of Contents

## Introduction

# Let the Healing Begin

I t's 4:00am on December 30, 2017, day four of my climb toward the 19,341-foot summit of Mount Kilimanjaro (Kili) in Tanzania, the highest point in Africa. I woke early due to the intestinal parasite quickly replicating inside of my digestive tract. Begrudgingly, I got dressed, wishing I could remain curled in the warmth of my sleeping bag instead of braving the cold air that looms at the dead of night in high altitudes. Planning to get back to my tent as quickly as possible, I wasn't prepared for the beauty of the night. As I emerged from my tent, the sky was astonishing. I whispered, "Wow." There wasn't a cloud in the sky. And while I couldn't see the moon, the stars looked bigger than they had the night before. It was like seeing glistening Christmas lights in the night sky.

The cramp in my intestines didn't allow me to stand in awe for very long as I hurried to the bathroom. Afterwards, I returned to view the sky. I was so taken aback by the experience that I sat down on a rock to take in the view before me. I was so awestruck that I whispered aloud, "Thank you God for this experience." As soon as the words escaped my lips, a shooting star flashed across the sky right in front of me. I hadn't seen a shooting star since I was a child growing up in the Adirondack Park in New York and could hardly believe this magical moment of the Universe responding to me. Tears started to well up in my eyes as I was overwhelmed with gratitude. As a tear rolled down my cheek, the streak of moisture brought my attention back to the cool, crisp air. I took a deep breath, smiled, and retreated to my tent for a few more hours of rest before we continued our trek toward the summit.

This was my second attempt at climbing Kili. During my first attempt, I got very sick and, on top of that, my climbing team was far from ideal. Having a second opportunity at a summit with a team that supported my journey made me feel fortunate the first attempt wasn't successful. During the second attempt, I was the only climber and had a team of nine people helping me to successfully summit the mountain: my guide, Prosper; my chef, Faustine; and seven amazing porters. I was actually the first person that day, January 2, 2018, to summit the mountain. Other climbers we passed warned us to slow down or we wouldn't make it. When I passed them again on the way back and told them I had already summited, they were shocked. Even the guides were shocked. I ate the most amazing meals and was surrounded by the most generous souls. I was truly blessed by the experience.

Being the only hiker, I spent a lot of time chatting with my team. Faustine, the chef, acknowledged my cheerful disposition multiple times during the trip. He confided in me, "Everyone is so happy that you're happy all of the time." He said most Americans always seem so unhappy as he demonstrated their typical look by slightly rounding his upper back, rolling his shoulders forward and mimicked a facial expression that appeared to be a combination of sad and upset. He said the entire group has felt very fortunate to be guiding me because it can be difficult working with people who look unhappy all the time.

What people often notice about me is my smile and cheerful, bubbly nature. What people, like my climbing team on Kili, generally don't know about me is how many times circumstances conspired to try to make joy an inaccessible emotion for me to experience. In my life, I've experienced multiple sexual violations from my childhood to late teens; have been attacked at knifepoint; found my significant other, Stan, dead when I was only 25 years old; and contemplated suicide numerous times. Through all those traumas and setbacks, I learned to hold on to the joy in my life. In fact, I'm often amazed at our resilience as humans as I'm proof you can not only heal from trauma but grow from it. It's possible to experience life in such beautiful ways, like I did on Kili, despite the periods of darkness.

I've experienced some of the worst that this world has to offer, but I've also experienced some of the best. Since my traumas, I've had tremendous life experiences. I've stood on top of the steep sea-cliffs in the Dingle Peninsula in Ireland that are met by the crashing waves of the turquoise Atlantic Ocean. I've enjoyed a gondola ride in Venice next to a man singing and playing the accordion on the same night as a total lunar eclipse. During a conservation project, I witnessed a sea turtle dig her nest and lay about 100 eggs in Costa Rica. I trekked around the majestic Kamchatka Peninsula, covered in volcanoes, bubbling hot springs, and gushing geysers. I flew through the sky like a bird when paragliding in the Caucasus Mountains.

Throughout this book, I'll share stories from my life. I'll be sharing some stories from my traumatic experiences, but I won't be going too deep into any of them. My goal is to not bring you into the depths of my despair and keep you there. But I'll let you look down into the hole I was in, so you can watch how I got myself out. The hope is that you'll learn ways to help yourself when you're also in the depths of despair.

As you move through the book, you'll learn that healing from trauma isn't easy and can be a lengthy and painful process. But what I'm hoping you'll learn from this book is that the personal growth you can experience along the healing journey can be beautiful. Embrace the journey. Don't spend your days wishing that the trauma never happened. That will keep you stuck in a past that cannot be changed. Instead, think of the many ways you can reinvent yourself. Think of what struggles you've made it through and how that proves just how strong you are. Realize that if you're still here after your trauma, you can make it through anything. I've used my traumas to prove to myself that I'm unstoppable. It has taken time to get to this point but being able to love the person I've become in the process has made the time and struggle worth it. My hope is that by the end of this book, you'll feel that you can also reach the same level of confidence, determination, and perseverance I've reached. Life will continue to test you, just like it has me. But by filling your toolbox with tools I'll present in later chapters that you can use when life throws you another blow, you'll see that you're strong enough to get up and keep moving forward, even after getting knocked down.

Trauma overwhelms our internal capacity to cope, so it's important to have a set of tools to use when overwhelmed. At various points in my life, I've used different tools for relief when healing from trauma. My hope is that if you feel like life is drowning you under the immense weight of all the pain it has to offer, you'll find ways to stay afloat and eventually reach land.

This book won't cover every type of technique that has ever been shown to be slightly effective in helping people overcome trauma. Instead, I'll share techniques that have helped me to cope with my own traumas and how you can apply them in your own life. The trauma healing process will be different for everyone. What works for one person may not work for another. And, by no means, should all the tools be used at the same time.

In addition to these tools, family bonds, friendship, and having a sense of community are all important in the healing journey. However, the major focus of this book is to teach you ways to heal and be happy on your own. It's nearly impossible to have healthy, mutually beneficial relationships unless we can learn to take care of ourselves first.

As a college professor, I've spoken to many students over the years about their anxiety. I offer them tips and tricks to provide them with some relief. One night an anxious student came to me after class and we talked for about 45 minutes. She explained she had a C at midterm and was worried about maintaining that C through the end of the semester. She told me about working a full-time job and taking 16 credits during the semester. She went on to tell me she was doing all this so she could graduate at the end of that semester and immediately move out of her parent's house.

The first question I asked her was what she does to take care of herself and help reduce her anxiety. She confided in me that she takes medication to help her anxiety and sees a therapist. Thankfully, she didn't say, "nothing," which is a very common response I get when I ask this question. However, she still used medication, which doesn't require her to do the internal work it takes to get through the difficult periods of her life. Please don't get me wrong; there's nothing wrong with using therapy and medication to help deal with difficult emotions. In fact, I've used both myself! But both require an intervening external force and discourage you from self-regulating your own disruptive thoughts, emotions, or impulses. Yes, under extreme stress, medication and therapy have been shown to increase one's chances of self-regulation.

Personally, I started taking medication so I could better handle talking about my trauma with a therapist. But I didn't start regularly seeing a therapist for a few more years after that because the medication took enough of the edge off of my anxiety and depression that I thought it wasn't necessary to talk to anyone. Then, when I finally did start talking to a therapist, I was eventually told that I would never be healed until I was ready to accept God into my life. Then the next therapist said that I would never be healed until I talked thoroughly about all my traumas. The process of reliving my trauma only sent me into a tailspin each time I had a session.

While I could have written off therapy as unhelpful, I persisted in searching for the right person. Therapy became successful for me when I found a therapist who didn't feel the need to go into the nitty-gritty details of each traumatic event in my life. Instead, we focused on my current life, future goals, and talked about how my past was interfering with my current life. Once I started to see how my traumas were keeping me back in my current life, my need for therapy and medication started to decrease.

I still see a therapist from time-to-time. Just like others, there are still times in my life that are really difficult. During these times, sometimes, I make the decision to go back on a low dose of Celexa to keep my anxiety and depression at bay. But I've learned how to cope in my daily life without feeling like I need to call my therapist every time life becomes overwhelming for me. I don't have the need to pop a Xanax when life becomes too difficult to bear. I've learned how to use breathing techniques, meditation, and yoga to help balance my emotions in my daily life. And from this book, you will too!

It's better to be able to tell yourself you're capable than depending on someone else to tell you. What happens when that person goes away or when no one else is around? You feel lost and out of sorts. It's common for people to look for something or someone outside of themselves to help ease the pain, but it's better if you can learn to help yourself.

It's empowering to know you're in control of your own happiness and how you react to uncomfortable situations. It's empowering to have the resources to turn to when you're feeling overwhelmed.

It's impossible to be happy every day, especially if you're using things outside of your own self to find that happiness. Think about it. When do you usually say that you're having a bad day? It most likely is when someone acted in a way you didn't like, or something happened that was out of your control. Every time we put our happiness in the hands of someone or something else, we give happiness and our power away.

What are you going to do when you're feeling overwhelmed and your significant other, parent, or friend is unavailable to take your call or your therapist isn't available to see you until next week or next month? We all have our own coping strategies such as drugs, alcohol, shopping, etc. Each of us has a standard go-to for releasing the pain, anxiety, and tension.

For me, I turned to food or harming my body. But I also relied on the men in my life to make me feel whole. And while they kept shattering my spirit, I remained steadfast in my belief that they made me whole. When doing some serious self-reflection, I realized I felt that Stan was the man who saved me when I was first feeling suicidal, so I felt I needed to find another man like him to replicate what I had lost when he was gone.

I used to write letters to Stan in my journal. In an entry I wrote on November 4, 2009, I was telling him how hard I was trying to let go of a guy who reminded me a lot of him. "I'm just so broken and I wish you were here to make me whole again. I think that's why I struggle with letting go of Roger; he reminds me so much of you that it's like he's my only chance of being whole again. Of course, in my heart of hearts I know this isn't true. But I can't help what I feel sometimes."

I've always looked for others, especially men, to make me feel important and that I matter. But I've come to realize that the only person I need to matter to is me. I can be there for myself in ways that others, like my significant other, cannot. Even though relationships are important, you need to be able to thrive independently of companionship and someone to lean on. During the early stages of trauma healing, support networks are extremely important; however, eventually, you'll have to let go of the support and learn you're capable of walking on your own. It's equally important to seek out resources during your times of need. Ease yourself into being able to self-regulate your emotions and difficult experiences in life without having to have another by your side during the entire journey. Life is hard and loss is an unfortunate part of it. By becoming dependent on another person for your happiness, it's a hard landing when, at some point, they're gone.

Because I relied on Stan for my happiness, I was devasted when he passed. Not only that, I expected to find someone else who could show me my own worth, when they may haven't even been capable of doing that. The men I dated after Stan were in just as much pain as me. So, how could they show me love and appreciation when they didn't even feel that they were deserving of love and appreciation themselves? It's essential that you're able to show others how you deserve to be treated. Don't allow someone else to determine how you should be treated. How on Earth could I expect anyone else to show me I matter when I've gone most of my life not believing in myself and thinking I'm insignificant?

I've seen this in my more recent relationships. In my quest to have men make me feel like I matter, I inadvertently make them feel like they don't matter. I act poorly toward them based on my beliefs about how they should make me feel. When they didn't show me love and affection the way I thought they should, I accused them of being unjust or unkind and would, in turn, punish them with hurtful words or actions. We give our power away when we expect others to make us feel a certain way. It also anchors in our mind the idea that we're unworthy or undeserving of love and affection when another person is unwilling or unable to fill the void we haven't learned how to fill ourselves.

Throughout life, we're always looking for someone else to take care of us. Our parents, significant other, teachers, therapists, or religious leaders, but what happens when no one is there? We feel lost. If you don't go out on your own, you'll never learn the skills you need to find contentment. It's empowering to become independent, to do something on your own, even though you're scared. Little by little, you start expanding your boundaries. The box you've created around yourself to protect you begins to open. You'll be amazed at how much more of life you can experience when you feel confident in yourself.

People are often shocked by how many life experiences I've had at a young age and the fact that I travel the world by myself. It's because I truly feel I can accomplish anything. I know it's true because I'm continually pushing my limits. I don't always succeed on my first try, nor do I expect initial success. Sometimes, it takes multiple times for me to be successful. I use the fact that I've made it through so many traumas to make me feel invincible. No matter what, I can make it through whatever life throws at me and come out stronger on the other side.

It's so easy to become overwhelmed by how hard life can be and all we have endured. But with just a minor shift in perspective, we can look at all we've been through to see how powerful and strong we actually are.

I went from being depressed, suicidal, promiscuous, bulimic, and drowning in financial debt to completing my PhD, being financially secure, exploring 45 states in the United States and 5 different continents, and now helping others work through their own healing journey. I want you to find your glimmer of hope. If I can feel so broken and bogged down by the darkness and come out on the other side feeling an immense love, excitement, and appreciation for life, it's possible for you too.

I spent so many years not understanding why I had to experience so much hardship in my life, wishing it never happened, wishing I had had an easier road. But without those experiences, I wouldn't be the same person I am today, nor would I have had the same amazing experiences.

The word "serotiny" holds a lot of significance for me. As a biology professor, my love of science and nature directly tie in with my feelings of strength and change into a single word which encapsulates my business, Serotinous Life. Serotinous cones only release their seeds when exposed to an environmental trigger, such as fire or death of the parent plant.

I like to compare us and our traumas to the Giant Sequoias, which are a type of serotinous tree that are endangered in California. Believe it or not, humans almost protected the largest trees on Earth into extinction. In an effort to protect these beautiful giants, conservationists prevented naturally occurring forest fires from moving through national parks to preserve these iconic trees. What we didn't previously know was that the trees required fire to open up their cones and release their seeds. So, without fires, their seeds never released, and new sequoias weren't allowed to germinate and replace the older generations that eventually started to die off.

Serotiny is analogous to our lives in many ways. People often only look at how destructive fires can be. They only look at what perished as a result of the fire or the devastation that was left behind. Most people don't realize that fires are very important in natural environments. Fires allow for new growth and new opportunities.

I believe we all have the seeds of greatness within us ready to spring forth and be brought to life. The fires of our past don't destroy us, they merely transform us and allow for new growth and life to spring forth. Just like forest fires cause serotinous cones to open, allowing for massive growth to follow, so does our trauma. It creates a space for us to grow as long as we're able to heal and move forward.

I reframed what I was telling myself about my trauma. I used to tell myself I was broken, and I couldn't be fixed. Then I recognized that I survived. I'm still here and the trauma is over. I made it through; and if I can make it through all that, I can make it through anything. Once I realized this, I started to challenge myself more with bigger adventures and climbing taller mountains. As I pushed my body physically, it also required me to be strong mentally. As I pushed my body and mind, both became stronger. As I kept pushing my perceived limitations, I realized I could conquer anything. It made me realize that healing is possible and that my life wasn't over.

I'm not special or unique. But I'm committed to the idea of not letting my perpetrators have any more control over me. I extended my victimization long after the events occurred by continuing to let it influence my thoughts, behaviors, actions, and ultimately, my life. Now, I refuse to let my traumas continue to control my life. I realized I was in control of my body and mind. I also realized that since I was strong enough to make it through sexual violations and the loss of my companion, then I'm strong enough to weather any storm.

I used several different tools to build the strength, courage, and independence I always had housed within me but didn't tap into. Hopefully, these tools will empower you along your journey as well. You deserve to feel comfort, to feel safe, and to feel that you're in charge of your life. You deserve to have hope. Healing is possible; never let anyone tell you different.

Dr. James S. Gordon eloquently states, "Pain, like death, will visit us all."[1] What matters is responding to ourselves with empathy and compassion, just as we would do for others. We must acknowledge when we're hurt rather than ignoring or minimizing our pain. The coming chapters will help shine a light into the areas of your life that are in deep need of love, kindness, empathy, and compassion. Please allow that light to shine through. Don't dim the light or turn it off because you don't think you're worthy of healing and happiness.

Healing from trauma is a long, arduous process, but the journey transforms you. How can you not be transformed by learning to listen to your body as well as processing thoughts and emotions without becoming incapacitated by them?

The tools in this book can be used to tackle the regular stresses of life that challenge your ability to stay focused at work, at home, and within your relationships. Use these techniques to hold on to your joy as well as create lasting changes that bring about a better quality of life. If life currently feels unbearable, there's a light ready to shine within you.

Please believe that hope and healing are possible.

# Chapter 1

# Goal Setting After Trauma

The thought of telling everyone I didn't successfully summit Ojos del Salado (Ojos), the tallest, active volcano in the world, scared me immensely. But, the more I thought about it, what really bothered me most was the thought of other people judging me based on my failure. This was the second big mountain I spent a lot of time and money to climb and failed to summit; first Kili and now Ojos.

In all reality, it didn't actually bother *me* that I didn't summit. I made the choice to turn back at 6,500 meters (21,325 feet). It was the highest I've ever climbed. But I was having to stop and catch my breath after every 5 to 10 steps I took. I felt it was a good decision for me to turn back when I did. My energy was severely depleted, and I needed to have some energy left to get back down the mountain. I stopped continuously to rest and catch my breath. To be honest, even if I had made it to the summit, there was no way I could have ever made it back down to base camp the same day.

Climbing that high on my own two feet was a success for me. I was also able to successfully summit my first 6,000-meter peak, Volcano San Francisco, which was an acclimatization hike before

Ojos. I felt great about that. However, even though I was happy about summiting my first 6,000-meter peak and reaching an elevation of 6,500 meters on Ojos, neither was a particularly enjoyable experience. I struggled with the altitude every day during the acclimatization process. We did our summit push one day early on Ojos because of weather conditions, so it's not surprising I ran into trouble on summit day. I constantly struggle with chronic back issues. Breaking down camp and setting it back up multiple times during the climb, quite frankly, sucked. This process coupled with carrying a 35-pound backpack caused a flareup of my back pain, which became worse the night before our summit attempt. Frustration also set in as multiple times a day I fought with the zippers on my tent just to get them open and closed. All the dust makes it impossible to keep the zipper tracks clear of debris. After 12 grueling days of this, I determined being trapped in a blistering hot tent, as you struggle frantically to open the zipper so you can get a breath of fresh air, could be used as an effective form of mental torture.

I was overwhelmed by the extreme heat from the desert and the huge gusts of wind that covered my body and all open orifices with a coating of dust. I constantly had the feeling of gritty sand in my mouth and was blowing out all sorts of nasty stuff from my nose. Coupled with that, I had a nagging cough that began on summit day, as my body tried to expel all the dust I had been inhaling for days. All these things exacerbated the stress my body was feeling from the altitude, which ultimately led to an unsuccessful summit attempt.

After my failed summit attempt on Ojos, the next day, I was provided with the option to climb another 6,000-meter peak. But I made the decision not to. Part of it was because of my back, but part of it was just because I knew it wouldn't be enjoyable. It would just be another volcano, with no path. Traipsing up a mound of rocks and dust, hoping you don't roll your ankle on one of the millions of little wobbly rocks, dust flying up in the air with every step and being blown around further by the strong gusts of wind that we had no protection from besides the layers of clothes we had on us, which protected us from the sun but roasted us in the process. None of that sounded enjoyable to me. Saying "No, I'm not going to climb that mountain because it offers me a 'do-over'" was a huge step for me. I didn't need to prove anything to myself or anyone else. I knew I wouldn't find the climb enjoyable, so I wasn't going to do it just to prove that I'm capable of climbing high mountains to someone else.

Please don't get me wrong; the whole climb wasn't horrible. I got to soak in the hot springs at Laguna Verde, which provided me with a little slice of heaven in the harsh desert. I got to see wild vicuñas and guanacos (both belong to the same family as camels, just like alpacas), foxes, and flamingos. I was shocked to see any form of life in such a barren desert. I enjoyed spectacular views, including a rainbow like I've never seen before as we were leaving Ojos base camp on New Year's Day. Instead of the rainbow having distinct bands of color, it covered a wide area of the sky. I saw explosions of red, orange, yellow, green, blue, and purple. The colors spread through the sky with uneven edges with one color merging into the next like God's fingerpainting. These are my most treasured moments from my 12 days in the Atacama Desert, and I'm so grateful for each experience.

But I had to ask myself, do I really want to keep attempting to climb the world's biggest mountains? That's not why I started climbing mountains in the first place.

When I was 24, I fell in love with Stan, a man twice my age, who saved my life and he didn't even know it. He loved me more than I loved myself. When I was around him, he made me feel beautiful, desirable, and like I deserved to have the world at my feet. The problem was, he was an addict, alcoholic, and ex-con who was on life parole. But I didn't care. Stan was a wonderful cook and he knew the way to my heart was through my stomach. Just to see me smile, he would make the most amazing meals. I would often open the door to go to work or to go check my mail to find flowers on my doorstep, just because. A random card would grace my pillowcase to remind me how much he loved me. He would even massage my feet and paint my toenails afterwards.

He never knew the traumas of my past. No one did. I'm sure he pieced some of it together when he'd find me crying and having almost a whole box of used tissues heaped up on the floor. He knew I had a story that I wasn't ready to tell. Stan would just hold me, tell me he loved me, and he knew I would tell him when I was ready.

After just a few times of people not believing me, telling me it was my fault, telling me I should be grateful that someone actually wanted to touch me, or that I should just grow up and get over it, I learned to just keep my mouth shut about my traumas. But I saw how it was all playing out in my life. Even when I chose not to acknowledge that the traumas even happened, they impacted my life nonetheless. I knew I had to address these issues, but I didn't think I was strong enough to handle admitting all those things actually happened to me in real life.

Once we decided to buy a house together, I knew Stan would be there for me over the long term. That's when I felt safe enough to begin acknowledging the traumas that happened in my past. So, even though a few weeks earlier I had just started my PhD program, I sought out a therapist to begin the healing process. I waited for a couple days after my first appointment to talk to Stan about my decision to go into therapy. The same day I decided to tell him about the traumas I was starting to address, his mom was diagnosed with terminal cancer. His mom meant so much to him, so how could I now burden him with my past? I couldn't. So, to continue the trend of keeping my secrets to myself, I decided to wait to tell him.

Not long after she was put in hospice, she died with Stan and I by her side. Not surprisingly, his mother's death hit him hard. As I watched Stan fall apart, I was dying inside. He was my strength and stability. Unbeknownst to him, I was reliving traumas I had buried deep for years. I felt I had no one I could trust with the knowledge of my past. I never thought things could get any worse until the day I walked in to find Stan dead. My whole world came crashing down at that very moment. As if that wasn't enough, a week and a half after finding him dead, I closed on the house we were supposed to be moving into together on the same day my first semester ended for my PhD program.

All these events sent me into a downward spiral. I was now living in a house, by myself, thinking about the life I was supposed to be living with a man who loved me in ways I never imagined. I couldn't walk anywhere in the house without thinking about the plans we made for each room. For solace, I started sleeping with one man after another as I sought other men like Stan, with the hopes of replicating what I had lost. I started to overeat and put on weight like crazy until I reached 222 pounds. Quickly adding on so much extra weight caused stretch marks to sprout across my belly like visible roots from the trauma taking hold of my body.

For the first few years, my doctor was patient with me and didn't give me too hard of a time for putting on the weight. That was until my cholesterol started to increase. I wasn't even 30 yet and I was diagnosed with high cholesterol. Something had to change. But I couldn't muster up the motivation to go to the gym. I had to find a way I could be physically active and enjoy what I was doing.

I started looking into Meetup groups, thinking that being around other people would be good for me and a few hiking groups caught my eye. I like to walk. I love being in nature. Why not try hiking, I thought? I started out with small hikes on trails in local parks that included walking over some hills. With being morbidly obese, going over these little hills felt like climbing Mount Everest.

I talk to all kinds of people and generally love getting to know them, so during these Meetups I would ask people why they were doing these hikes. I got a lot of the same answers: to meet other people, get out of the house, or be healthy. But there was one answer that intrigued me the most. One woman said she was getting ready to meet her goal of climbing Mount Marcy. Seeing as I had never heard of this mountain, I asked her about it. She proudly told me it's the highest mountain in New York. That night I researched Mount Marcy and saw it was part of a list of mountains called the Adirondack 46. The 46 highest mountains in the Adirondack park.

This was my turning point, my moment to finally start growing into the woman I longed to be. I'm such a goal-oriented person, lists are right up my alley. This list of mountains finally gave me something to work toward. A goal I wanted to accomplish for myself and not because someone else thought it was best for me. This is when I decided I wouldn't exercise just to be healthy, but I would exercise to meet a goal.

From that point on, I started hiking over 100 mountains every year. I finished one list after another then set my sites on even bigger lists, which sent me trekking throughout the world. The mountains became the places where I felt most at peace and where I first began to heal. They're where I found my inner strength and, through that journey, transformed my mind, body, and soul. But in the process of climbing bigger and bigger mountains, my body was starting to break down, and I was enjoying each climb less and less.

By the time I had gotten to Ojos, I had been soul searching for some time on my mountaineering goals. My reflection began 5 months earlier during my 33-day trip throughout Russia. Traveling East to West through this amazing country was the most spectacular experience of my life. Climbing Mount Elbrus, the highest point in Europe, wasn't even close to being my favorite part of the trip. If I'm brutally honest, it was actually one of the least favorite parts of my trip. I was just afraid to tell the world I didn't enjoy it because that climb was my main mission for traveling to Russia in the first place. Then, I took a trip to Chile where the best parts for me were, again, outside of the climb. The trip to Chile really solidified for me that I wanted to climb mountains and do treks known for being beautiful and enjoyable, not just because they're on a list of impressive mountains to climb.

I started climbing mountains to heal and to reexperience happiness, but, instead, my joints ached worse, and I became increasingly miserable with each climb.

I had set my sights on climbing Kili and Elbrus because my goal was to climb the seven summits, the highest point on each continent. But during the climbs of Elbrus and Ojos, I started asking myself, do I really want to spend two months climbing Mount Everest? Do I really want to carry a 50-pound pack and drag a 50-pound sled up and down Mount Denali? Do I really want to set up and break down camp time and time again? Do I want to spend a small fortune to put myself through all these hardships, just to prove I can do hard things? The answer was a resounding NO to each of these questions. I already know I can make it through hard things. I know I'm much happier sleeping in a bed and being able to shower and shave. I know I can have significantly more experiences by spending less money on shorter climbs plus I get to travel to even more countries and do more while I'm there.

At Ojos, I truly felt the Universe put the other two climbers in my group with me for a reason. Chie and Pedro, who I'm very happy to report, were both able to summit Ojos del Salado, even though I had to turn back. Chie is an attorney from Japan who completed the seven summits, and is now working on the second seven summits, the second highest point on each continent. I feel the Universe put her in my path so I could learn what it's like to climb the seven summits. Pedro is an economist from Portugal, who has traveled to more countries than any person I've ever met before. I feel the Universe put him in my path at the same time of Chie's so I could learn there are so many other countries to visit and treks I can do that can be even more magical than the seven summits. Pedro inspired me with stories of exotic adventures around the world and provided me with numerous examples of some of the most magical places on Earth that I should visit.

It's important to be flexible with our goals. Two of my big ones were to be on Mount Everest on my 40th birthday and to finish the seven summits. But what I realized is I don't want to achieve those goals any longer. Through self-reflection, I've come to realize that traveling through different countries and experiencing different places, people, and food is what I love most about my adventures abroad, not the mountains I climb.

I also want to open my trips up to new adventures like scuba diving. My favorite experience during my trip to Russia was paragliding, which has always been on my bucket list. I only have so much time and financial resources for traveling every year. So, if I keep dedicating these resources to climbs with ever-increasing expense and duration, I won't have as many of these resources available for other mind-blowing experiences. Taking the seven summits off my bucket list takes a lot of financial pressure off of me. Just climbing these seven mountains costs around $200,000, and that's only if I'm successful on the first shot for each one. That money can surely buy me a lot more than just seven adventures.

Declaring your goals to the world is important to create accountability for yourself. But keep in mind, it's perfectly acceptable to change paths if the path you're on no longer works for you. Dr. Tom Morris said in *The Seven Greatest Success Ideas,*

> Too many people seem to be busy chasing the wrong
> things, rushing down a road that's really not right for them.
> They feel somehow dissatisfied. They don't want to give

up. I mean, who wants to labeled a quitter? But they can't tolerate things as they are, so in an effort to improve matters, they increase their pace. But what good is running faster in the wrong direction?[2]

That's why it's important to regularly reevaluate your goals, determine if you're on track to meet your goals, and decide if adjustments need to be made, which includes deciding if a change of course is necessary. You aren't stuck on that path because you said that's what you initially wanted to do. Don't worry about what people will think and say. I've changed paths many times in my life and each time, it has proven to be for the best. The key is I didn't remain stagnant after I shifted paths, I moved onto an even more exciting and fulfilling path.

It's important to distinguish between giving up on a goal because it's hard versus giving up on a goal because it's not actually giving you the happiness you were looking to achieve from it. I now know if I were to continue to pursue these long expeditions, I wouldn't be doing it because I actually wanted to. I would be doing it to save face and not let people think I'm backing down from my goal because it's hard. I'm not backing down; I'm just altering my course to put me on a much more enjoyable path. We're able to design our life, but we have to regularly check in with ourselves to see if the path is still the one we want to be on. That's why checking in with your goals regularly is so important. Being able to make alterations, if necessary, is one of the keys to living a healthy life.

You might be thinking to yourself, *I just want to make it through my day, and she wants me to be setting goals?* First, having goals to work toward, even just to brush my teeth that day, was, hands down, the most important part of my healing journey. Second, I believe that having goals to work toward will also be the most important part of *your* healing journey. Goal-setting is a critical component of The BOSS Technique I created to help my clients work through their trauma.

The BOSS Technique helps people to harness, manage, or overcome stress. There are four main components: Balance, Outcome specification, Self-talk, and Self-care. Balance occurs when you decide enough is enough and you take back control of your life. Outcome specification utilizes the neuro-linguistic programming (NLP) process of getting very specific about your goals. NLP is a powerful technique I've studied to help my clients work through their limiting beliefs and negative Self-talk. And finally, Self-care, is rooted in the belief you deserve love, kindness, and compassion. This is a critical component of healing from trauma which often gets overlooked.

There's a reason you chose to read this book. And there's a change you want to make in your life. Your *goal* is to make a change. Goals don't have to be enormous, insurmountable obstacles like Everest. Your goal could simply be getting out of bed each morning. I've been there. In fact, at one point in my life, my goal for the day was to take a shower. Other days, my goal was to take out the trash. On others, it was to not sleep with another strange man. But some of my goals were larger, to get my Ph.D., to summit huge mountains, and to travel to different exotic locations. But my goals weren't always big and extravagant. Some were simply around getting through one day at a time; to just take one more step because we always have one more step in us.

For my new friend, Dee, the idea of always being able to take one more step transformed her life. It was the first-time Dee had ever been in a rock-climbing gym and she was only going about halfway up the wall each time before coming back down. After watching her climb a few times, I reached out to talk to her.

I asked, "What's holding you back? Because, I'm going to be honest and tell you, I think you can make it to the top."

She replied, "You know what it is; I broke my ankle a few years ago, and I'm worried about reinjuring it."

I asked, "How many years ago did you injure your ankle?"

After thinking for a moment, she said, "Maybe five or six years ago."

I smiled and excitedly answered, "Let me tell you something, I teach anatomy and physiology. You're healed. You're fine! Your body can handle it. You can put all of your weight on that ankle and it's going to be fine."

Dee started laughing. Then after a moment, she said, "You know what I think I could do? If I taped my ankle, I think I could do it then."

I looked at her with a puzzled look and replied, "But does your ankle hurt? Like right now, does it hurt?"

"No."

"When you're climbing, does it hurt?"

"No."

"Then there's no reason to tape your ankle. The only reason you would tape your ankle is to make you feel safe mentally, like you have protection. But I'm going to tell you that physically you don't need it. Do you know what's going to help you more than anything? It's for you to get up on that wall, put all your weight on that ankle, stand up on the foot holds and see that it's fine. That's when you're going to be able to move on. So, tonight, get on that wall one more time and put all of your weight on that ankle."

She looked dismissively and said, "Maybe I will."

After a few minutes of us watching other climbers, I nudged her by saying, "How about it? Let's you and me go back over, and you try it."

Dee reluctantly agreed, so we walked over to the wall. As we did, I was asking her if she felt her legs or arms were stronger. She replied her legs.

I said, "Think about what's happening. You're afraid to put your weight on that foot, so you're depending on your arms. You need to trust your feet and legs and start putting weight on them, so you stop tiring out your arms."

Once we got to the wall, she started climbing. I'm talking her through about where she's going to go next. At halfway up, she said, "This is where I got tired before and always stop."

"Just rest," I said. Since she was in a corner, I told her to lean forward and rest. Just let her arms down and hang so they could rest and she could keep going. She takes a moment to rest and then keeps going up. When she was just about a foot away from the top, I yelled to her, "You just need one more step. One more step and you're going to reach the top!"

Dee said, "I don't have one more step."

With a power in my voice, I said, "We always have one more! We can always take just one more step!" I repeated, "One more step," and that's what she did. She lifted her leg up, put her weight on it, stood up, and hit the top of the wall. The pride in her was immediately apparent. You could see her light up and she screamed, "I made it! I made it! I hit the top!" Immediately after, she said, "I want to come down." But then she quickly stopped and said, "No, I can't come down; I have to show everyone. So, she yelled to her friends around the corner, "Come see this!" All her friends rushed over and couldn't believe she was at the top. Everyone started taking pictures and congratulating her. I could see the pride radiating out of her.

After I belayed her down, Dee gave me a huge hug and said, "I did it. I didn't believe that I had one more step, but you're right; we always have one more step in us." It was amazing to watch her push beyond her perceived limitations. I explained, "Our bodies are amazing. What limits us most isn't our body but our mind. Our mind limits almost everything in our lives."

What really limits you all the time are things you tell yourself about what you can and cannot do, what's possible and what's not. Anything you put your mind to is possible. Sometimes, you may reach your goal the first time around, but there's success in even just trying. Each time you're going to get just a little bit better, a little bit stronger, a little more skilled, and, eventually, you'll reach your goal, as long as you keep trying. If you stop trying, you'll never reach the top of the rock wall or the top of that mountain. If you give up, if you're unwilling to take one more step, you're never going to reach the position title, career, travel destination, or whatever your goal is. Most of the time, people give up because they limit themselves by their own perceived limitations, which, like Dee's ankle, aren't real. People don't really have as many limitations as they like to believe. It's amazing what you can do when you remove your self-imposed limitations.

It might seem contradictory to say don't give up on your goals after telling you a story of me giving up on some of my bigger climbing goals. But there's a difference between giving up on a goal because of limiting beliefs, versus giving up on a goal that's no longer serving you. As the popular saying goes, you don't want to get to the top of the ladder just to find that it's propped up against the wrong wall.

Examine your goals and determine if they're really what YOU want. Is someone else or society dictating what your goals should be? When my students aren't doing well in class and I know that they're not committing the necessary time to be successful, I ask them if they want to be doing this degree program and why they chose it in the first place. I commonly get answers like, "My parents told me I had to get a job or go to school, so I chose school," "I wanted to study art, but my friends and family told me that wasn't realistic and to get a job in healthcare where I could always find a job," or "My employer is requiring that I complete a higher degree or I'll lose my job."

Make sure your goals are based on what you want to achieve, not what someone else wants for you. Some people prefer to live vicariously through others. With my students, parents who didn't achieve specific goals often want to see their children reach those goals. When a goal isn't your own, you often lack motivation and interest in completing it.

People were so disappointed when I started stepping away from climbing big mountains and started to put my energy into yoga and growing my coaching practice. At first, I let it really get to me, seeing the sheer disappointment in their faces and the change in their body language after telling them. I had to remember they were responding that way because they were living vicariously through me. So, when I stopped my mountain adventures, it was as if I were stopping their mountain adventures too.

Many people who've experienced trauma identify themselves as an incest victim, combat soldier, or a survivor. Learning new skills can help you to learn a role that's different than the one you have learned how to play from your traumas. Achieving new goals helps you to find a new way of identifying yourself after your trauma.

When setting your goals, don't think in terms of what you think is possible or not possible. Set a goal that makes you happy, excites you, and could change the trajectory of your life. Self-doubt and insecurity are common, particularly with those of us who've experienced trauma. If you have trouble with doubting your ability to succeed, make a list of what you've been successful at in the past.

I created a running list in a notebook, but you can also use a document on your computer or phone. Creating a running list allows you to add to it over time as you continue to collect evidence that supports your capability of achieving your goals. Record every little success, every exam you passed, every bit of positive feedback you've received. I like to keep emails and cards people wrote to me acknowledging how I helped them or the great job I did. I make notes of text messages or comments I receive on social media that made me feel good. It's so easy to remember all the times you've failed. If you're shifting how you think, this is a way to collect evidence as tangible proof to yourself that you're amazing. In the depths of depression and despair, it's hard to access the positive in life. Keeping a tangible document or items helps to remind you of what's good about you when you can't easily access those feelings on your own.

I also encourage you to study others who've achieved what you want to achieve. As the late business philosopher, Jim Rohn would say, "If you wish to be successful, study success. If you wish to be happy, study happiness. If you wish to be wealthy, study wealth. Don't leave it to chance. Make it a study."[3] So, if your goal is to be able to overcome your trauma, study people who have overcome trauma. If you want to write a book, study successful authors. If you want to climb Mount Everest, study people who've successfully summited the mountain. In today's world, we have access to more information than ever. I encourage you to read or listen to books and podcasts and go to lectures and workshops so you can learn from people who've achieved what you want to achieve. Don't get paralyzed when trying to move forward with a new goal because you don't know where to begin. An abundant amount of information is out there that will outline the steps others have taken to achieve the same results you desire for yourself. You don't have to guess!

## Activity

As Mark Victor Hansen says, "By recording your dreams and goals on paper, you set in motion the process of becoming the person you most want to be. Put your future in good hands – your own."[4] Using a journal, notebook, or document on your phone or computer write down one goal that would make the biggest change in your life if you were to achieve it. The goal can be from any area of your life (e.g., health, finances, relationships, etc.). Choose a goal that will positively influence all or most other aspects of your life when you achieve it.

<u>Guidelines When Writing Your Goals</u>

1. **Be specific** – Don't just write, "I want to be happy." Define what being happy looks like to you. As Tom Morris said in *The Seven Greatest Success Ideas*, "Vague thoughts cannot motivate specific behavior."[2]

2. **Create measurable goals** – How will you know when you achieved your goal? Don't just write, "I want to lose weight." Losing one pound qualifies as losing weight but losing one pound is very different from losing 30 pounds. Be specific about how much weight you want to lose.

3. **Identify the time-frame** – When do you want to achieve your goal by? For example, "I want to start my own business one year from now" and identify that date.

4. **State your goal in the positive** – State your goal in terms of what you want to achieve versus what you want to avoid. For example, instead of writing, "I don't want to be broke at retirement," write, "I want to have $1 million in my retirement account so I can live comfortably."

5. **Be self-directed** – Your goal should be within your control. It shouldn't be based on another person doing or not doing something. Don't put your future in someone else's hands.

6. **Be realistic** – You don't want to set yourself up for failure. Your goals must be obtainable and reachable in the timeframe you've set for yourself. For example, don't say that you want to climb Mount Everest in six months when you've never climbed a single mountain in your entire life.

Once you have written your goal, place it somewhere that will help to motivate you. Maybe you want to keep your goal close to you in a wallet, or see it every day on your mirror. In any case, make sure you know where it is so you can be motivated to achieve it. And if at any time, that goal no longer serves your greater good, choose a different goal and set your sights on a different path.

# Chapter 2

# Habits to Replace

Throughout my life, I've put myself in so many dangerous situations due to bad habits. When I think of how many times I've been in situations where I was physically and emotionally hurt, I also have to think of how many times I've been spared from pain and even death. For example, I was casually sleeping with a guy who wanted me to bring him to a place. I offered to drive him there, but in the middle of the trip, he randomly switched to a different destination. It totally threw me for a loop, but when I stopped the car and spoke up saying "no," things got ugly. He looked at me, stuck out his tongue, and there was a hidden razor blade in his mouth. He casually took it off his tongue and said, "Drive." At that point, I decided to take him where he wanted to go because I was afraid of being harmed.

Another time, I was stranded in New York City late at night. The guy I was sleeping with and I headed into NYC to see some of his friends. I ended up stuck in an apartment with a bunch of random people while he proceeded to take all my money, drive off with my car, wreck it, and flee the scene of the crime. At this point, I had to leave the apartment to go to the police station and explain what had happened to the car. When I was done, it was clear I couldn't just stay at the station. I had nowhere to go. I didn't know anyone in the city. After walking into motel after motel inquiring about their rates, I ended up meeting a guy who was also looking for a cheap place to stay. We found a really inexpensive motel and split the cost of a really creepy room with the few dollars I was able to withdraw from my bank account at the ATM. While we had to sleep in the same bed, nothing sexual happened. I remain immensely grateful to this day that I wasn't hurt or killed that night. That was one of the lowest points in my life. While promiscuity had been a long-time habit of mine, after Stan died, I began to bring men into my life who were extremely dysfunctional. But I chose to bring them into my life rather than being forced to out of sheer necessity.

Most days, I was unable to work because I had fallen into such a deep depression. During this time, I started looking for men to pay my bills on Craigslist in exchange for sexual favors. Believe it or not, I was reported and banned from posting on Craigslist for a while because of my solicitous posts. I didn't post pictures of myself or come out and directly offer sex, but it was obvious what I was suggesting. I was at risk of financial ruin. I was sleeping with numerous men. So, I figured I might as well get financial rewards from passing out my body to any man who showed interest in me. I never ended up sleeping with men in exchange for financial favors. But knowing I got to the point where I would have still brings up a lot of shame inside of me.

I cannot begin to say how grateful I am to my mother for helping me financially during this time. In less than a year's time, she had given me over $20,000 to help me pay my bills. My mother didn't have a lot of money at the time, and she chose to skimp on what she needed to get by to help me. Even with this financial help I still had a lot of credit card debt, had creditors calling, and wasn't paying the property and school taxes on my home because I was spending so much money on food, drinking, and clothes to cover my ever-expanding waistline. I understand how easy it is for people to fall into a life of prostitution and drugs if they don't have supports in place to help them out. I was eventually able to repay my mother all the money she had loaned me after selling the house I had bought right after Stan died.

Another habit I've had for many years is picking at my skin. Numerous times, I've picked at my skin until it bled. With the blood came a feeling of release; something bad was finally being expelled from my body. Of course, picking at my skin led to more pimples and outbreaks that made me feel worse about myself, which made me feel like I had to pick even more. It was a vicious positive feedback cycle that seemed to have no end.

I've always had this deep desire to discharge all the disgust, hurt, and resentment from my body. If I weren't picking at my skin to remove any bumps caused by pimples or ingrown hairs, I would spend inordinate amounts of time trimming split ends out of my hair. I would have so much work to do and yet I would spend hours searching for split ends to cut out of my hair. Ultimately, it was also about removing an imperfection, one that I felt I had control over. To stop this habit, I decided to chop my hair off. That way, it wouldn't be accessible for me to obsessively trim split ends from.

The times between picking at my skin and trimming the split ends out of my hair would often be interspersed with bulimic purging, or exercising until I felt my body couldn't move anymore.

I wanted to release the contents of my stomach and burn every bit of fat off my body. It took me years to realize that by doing these things, I was trying to expel my traumas. My trauma was sprouting roots through my obsessive behavior. I was allowing it to stay grounded in every part of my being until I was ready to acknowledge what I was trying to rid myself of.

There isn't a single person on Earth who knows everything that happened to me. Some I don't even fully know myself. The ones that happened when I was young come in flashes to my memory and I often wonder if those things actually happened or if I made them up. Did I bury the pain because it was too hard to acknowledge? Have I been hurt so much that I have villainized every person from my past even if they never hurt me? It's hard for me to accurately pinpoint.

I was ashamed of the person I became after my traumas. The promiscuity, the eating disorder, and the many dangerous situations in which I chose to put myself in. Because of this, I always encourage my clients to work on forgiving themselves for the choices they have made since their trauma. In the documentary *Cracked Up: The Darrell Hammond Story*, Dr. Bessel van der Kolk said, "The most important thing is forgiveness of yourself, for having been as vulnerable, as scared, as angry, as frozen as you were. And forgiving yourself for all the ways you've tried to survive." He recognized, "That's a big job."[5]

It's imperative to recognize that you've done what you've done since your trauma simply to survive. Even though some days are still hard for me, it's becoming easier and easier to forgive myself and to embrace the strength and resiliency it took to stay standing with each progressively stronger blow that life threw at me.

I often felt broken. Often, I used the word "broken" to describe myself before I started to study neuro-linguistic programming (NLP). One of the presuppositions of NLP is that we're working perfectly. No one is broken. We acquired every habit and behavior for a reason. Even if it's not serving us in our current lives, that habit or behavior stuck around because it did serve us in the past. You'll never be able to change an undesirable behavior until you understand what you're gaining from that behavior and then find other ways to cope.

Drinking alcohol may help you to decrease anxiety, so if you want to stop drinking alcohol, you must determine how you're going to deal with that anxiety once alcohol is no longer an option. Maybe you started to take a stimulant drug like cocaine because you were so tired each day from your many sleepless nights. Memories creep into your dreams and prevent you from getting a good night's rest. You can't just stop taking a stimulant drug until you learn how to cope with those painful memories so they don't keep disturbing your sleep, or at the very least you must learn strategies for how to get back to sleep when the painful memories resurface in your dreams.

It's so easy for outsiders who have not experienced trauma, to look from the outside, wag their finger at you, and tell you that you shouldn't smoke, drink, overeat, take drugs, cut yourself, gossip, cry, complain, or be angry. They can't comprehend why you developed those habits in the first place. But, some of those habits might have actually saved your life. How could you just give something up that protected you or gave you a moment of relief from a painful existence? The answer is, you can't. You must determine why you developed that habit in the first place, and if it's still serving you, what can you replace it with? Replacement is why alcoholics sometimes turn to smoking after they stop drinking or why people who stop smoking might turn to sugar. It's just substituting one addiction for another because the underlying reason of how that behavior is still serving them hasn't been addressed. If you try to remove a habit that was an integral part of your coping system, it could be detrimental to remove that habit, even if it appears to be maladaptive, without replacing it with something else, especially if you haven't become fully aware of what triggers you to engage in that habit.

Some people manage their pain by starving themselves, taking drugs, or cutting themselves. I have a habit of seeking out sweets or just something unhealthy to put into my mouth when I'm wanting to avoid feeling a certain way. It allows me a way to escape uncomfortable feelings that arise.

I also have a habit of taking over-the-counter pain medicine whenever I feel the slightest bit of pain without really addressing why I'm in pain. Although I still have more work to do with this, I've learned to sit with my pain instead of trying to push it away with various medications. Pain is one of our body's alarms that directly tells us something isn't right. By sitting in silence with my pain, I noticed the pain medicine doesn't actually help, other than the placebo effect that's created by me trying to use an external force to solve an internal problem.

I used to pop Xanax any time I felt a little anxious or I would put a sugary snack in my mouth at the first sign of any uncomfortable feeling from depression, anxiety, or boredom. I would also find reasons to go shopping both online or in stores. Because of this, I acquired immense credit card debt as well as a lot of unnecessary items. I did all of this in a quest to obliterate my pain with more things that seemingly gave me momentary relief.

Then, I found caffeinated gum when I was in line at the grocery store. I actually didn't start using any form of caffeinated substance until I turned 36. After using the gum for a while, I discovered caffeinated mints, and I was hooked.

When I began to track the number of mints I put in my mouth each day, I realized I was taking 12-14 mints a day, the equivalent of 6-7 cups of coffee! After tracking the number of mints I was taking, I started to pay attention to what I was thinking and feeling right before I took one. An interesting finding for me was that I would take many mints prophylactically when I thought I was going to be tired versus when I was actually tired. This isn't surprising as I do the same thing with pain medicine. I also started to notice I felt more tired after I took the mint. This is why awareness is key to changing a habit. You can't change a behavior or habit that you don't fully understand. Once you start becoming aware of when you engage in the habit, then you can begin to understand it. It's important to fully understand when and where you engage in that habit, your behavior, and the trigger that precipitated it.

Another habit I had that took on multiple forms is the need to escape my current situation. I used to change jobs as soon as I became uncomfortable. I moved when I became uncomfortable. I left relationships because I was uncomfortable. Luckily, I have settled down in my jobs, homes, and relationships better now, but I still go through periods when I start coming up with reasons to leave or move.

I never really settled into any place until my most recent home. I always had boxes that I never unpacked. From many of my traumas, I acquired a fear of being trapped. I always felt scared of not being able to escape. So, I never got too comfortable in my home because I wanted the ability to leave whenever I felt stuck. I've done the same thing in my jobs and relationships. In my most recent long-term relationship, I spent most of our time together trying to get out of the relationship.

I would also try to escape my current life by going to another country. I became obsessed with planning one trip after another, so I always had a way to escape. This habit seemed to be good on the outside but stemmed from my trauma, so it was doing more harm than good in my life. It's a constant struggle, but I'm slowly learning to be happy wherever I am, whether at home, work, or traveling. Until you can learn to be happy in an uncomfortable situation, you'll find unhappiness wherever you go. The only person you have control over is yourself. No matter how many times you change jobs, homes, or significant others, you're going to end up back in the same place because you keep bringing the same person along, you. And the unhappiness is ultimately created by you. That was a hard pill for me to swallow, but I had to acknowledge I was never going to have better relationships, jobs, or satisfaction in my home until I changed what I thought and how I reacted to people and situations in my life.

For many years, I've been a proud workaholic. I used to feel that people harshly judged me, so I aimed to accomplish so much to prove everyone wrong. I pushed myself so hard to prove to myself and everyone else that I'm worthy, that I'm good enough, that I'm lovable. What I came to realize is the only real judgment I ever faced came from me. I also realized I was very judgmental of others, which was likely a reflection of the way I judged myself.

One of my students was studying to be a therapist due to her own traumatic history. She asked me if I thought it was necessary to delve into the trauma and divulge everything about it to move through it. After reflecting for a moment, I told her while I know there are different feelings and thoughts on how someone should move through trauma, through my own trauma history, I've found going through and reliving every little gritty detail was retraumatizing. So, I didn't think it was essential or necessary.

What's necessary, is to become aware and recognize where the trauma is playing itself out in your life. Most people are not aware how the trauma currently affects them even when they refuse to acknowledge it. With an addiction, it's unlikely that you'll be able to overcome the addiction until you see why you're turning to that substance in the first place. What are you trying to hide? What are you trying to keep down? What pain are you trying to numb?

Most people think they can't help themselves. Even if their body has a physiological desire to use, they don't realize that by sitting for a moment in quiet discomfort and trying to understand why they're needing to use at that moment, that they could find an alternative way to cope with the difficult feelings. Are they anxious? Are they sad? Are they excited? How are they feeling in their body and how are they feeling in their mind? What feelings are they wanting to avoid? What thoughts do they not want to think?

You're not going to stop using drugs, food, social media, sex, or any other negative habit unless you understand why you're doing it in the first place. Once you're ready to stop a bad habit or behavior, you must start recognizing when you want to engage in that behavior so you can stop it. Becoming aware of when you're wanting to engage in that habit will help you to release it. Sometimes, you may not even realize what's happening. That's why bringing awareness to the situation is paramount to ending the behavior. Awareness brings something that's in your subconscious to your conscious mind. Once you start becoming aware of when your past is reliving itself in your present life, you'll be able to change any habit. You'll be able to replace the habit with something else that's not so potentially destructive or harmful to your body, like moderate exercising, spending time with friends, or watching a movie that makes you laugh. There are things that you can do that will cause your brain to release the neurotransmitters, the special chemicals, that will make you feel good without turning to a substance or harmful activity.

One of my newest habits is spending at least two hours every day listening to personal and professional development audio. However, what I've come to learn is I've used it as a distraction to avoid difficult thoughts. A few years ago, I came home from The Body Keeps the Score workshop at the Kripalu Center for Yoga & Health. My boyfriend and I decided to watch the movie, *Saturday Night Fever*. It was the first time I had ever seen the movie. When I saw the girl crying and saying, "No" as she was being raped, I ran out of the room. I went upstairs and picked my face then put on an Unblemish face mask. When the scene was over, my boyfriend told me to come back, and we finished the movie together. After that, I went upstairs to finish my skincare routine. But I had forgotten my phone downstairs. Part of my routine is to listen to an audiobook while I'm washing my face. This time, I forced myself not to go get the phone because of how anxious I was feeling. I knew the reason I wanted to get my phone and listen to the audio was to avoid my current feelings. Around this time, I began to notice that I start feeling anxious when I don't have my phone on and I'm in silence. So, that night, after watching the movie, I told myself I was safe, and I wasn't being hurt. I was able to continue washing my face without going to get my phone. It was a huge success! Now I purposely have periods of time throughout the day when I'm in silence during my daily routines. This allows me the space I need to practice allowing difficult thoughts to come in and not let them stay and fester. This new habit of silence has helped me to find the healing energy of quiet.

Learning NLP helped me realize I'm not broken, and I don't need to be fixed. It opened my world and made me realize I don't need an external force to heal. I have all that I need to heal inside of me. I can control and change my habits, so I can create a new platform on which to stand. That's why I love being a life coach. It's about showing people that everything they need to heal from their traumas and succeed in all aspects of life is already inside of them. It was life changing to learn it myself and I love sharing that gift with others.

In the coming chapters, I'll share the ways I've learned to cope with my traumas that weren't self-injurious to replace my harmful habits. I'll share my traumas and my struggles along with ways I overcame and refocused my attention for a happier and healthier life. I hope it will give you ideas for what you can do when you're battling with gut-wrenching heartache that seems insurmountable.

Journaling, drawing, painting, writing poetry, dancing, and exercise, which will all be discussed in the coming chapters, can all offer forms of emotional release. Sometimes, the words are not accessible to describe how you're feeling in your journal or in a poem. In those cases, you might be able to express those feelings in colors or shapes in drawings or paintings. Sometimes the only form of release can be by expressing yourself through dance, walking, or going to the gym.

What may work for one difficult situation might not work for another. Because of this, the coming chapters will cover a variety of tools you can try out and see what fits. I encourage you to try each activity. You might be surprised by the relief it brings! Maybe you'll rekindle an old interest or find a new passion as you try the activities in the coming chapters. I invite you to approach each activity with an open mind. Remembering that you're just acquiring tools for your toolbox. Even if you don't continue to use it now, you might return to one of these activities in the future as your life circumstances change.

During these activities, you might feel emotions well up inside, or even start to cry. It's okay; just let it flow out naturally. It's not unusual to allow stress from our traumas to build up inside of us. When animals experience stress, they literally shake it off. They release it. As humans, we tend to intellectualize our experiences and try to work through our difficult emotions logically. But trauma and how it lives in our body cannot always be explained away by reason. Trying to make sense of traumatic circumstances that happened by pure chance or because of the behavior of another person that was completely out of your control is a lost cause. Sometimes, it just doesn't make sense and will never make sense, and we can drive ourselves to the brink of insanity or to the depths of despair trying to make sense of a tragedy that was completely out of our control. We must find a way to release the tension that gets stored in our body and move forward.

Continually replaying a trauma we had no control over perpetuates the feelings of being hopeless and helpless. We have to move through it. We have to learn to live in the present moment and move forward from a past that cannot be changed.

## Activity: Identifying and Replacing Harmful Habits

Sit in a quiet place where you can spend some time reflecting on your own habits. What have you done to help you cope with difficult situations and feelings in the past? What do you currently do to cope? Does it help you deal with the difficult emotions? Does it harm you in any way? Sometimes, what we choose as a coping mechanism can actually hurt us.

Take a piece of paper and draw three columns. Think about what habits you have that no longer serve you. Identify the habits and behaviors you want to change and write them down in the first column. Think about when these habits show themselves and write it next to each habit in the second column. Remember, building awareness is the first step to making a change! Next, write a healthier behavior to replace it with in the third column.

Look at the list of your current coping mechanisms. What would you like to keep and why? What do you want to get rid of and why? Don't plan to get rid of all your bad habits at once! Choosing all of them will only set you up for failure and ingrain your bad habits even more. Pick one to focus on for now, make the change, and then work on the others in the future.

# Chapter 3

# Meditation

I struggled with suicidal thoughts all through my 20s. When I was with Stan, these thoughts subsided. But after he died, they returned with a vengeance. While writing this book, I was shocked to find I had created a safety plan for myself in my journal:

Support/Safety Plan:
- If I'm feeling suicidal - force myself to get out of the house. Either go for a walk or drive.
- If I'm picking at myself or pulling/cutting my hair:
    - Take a deep breath.
    - Tell myself "You're in control of your actions and your life."
    - Take another deep breath.
    - Tell myself "You're beautiful and you don't need to hurt yourself."
    - Take another deep breath.
    - Stop whatever I'm doing and walk away for five minutes."

I spent a lot of my time depressed and living in the past. Once I started to heal, I transitioned to being anxious and focusing on my future. I began seeking goals to achieve such as to become rich and famous. This would allow me to finally be and feel seen, to feel like my existence mattered. That's when I began my habit of listening to 2-3 hours of personal and professional development audio each day. I listened while in my car, getting ready for work in the morning, and before bed at night. I still listen to about that much audio every day, but I try to incorporate more silence than I was at first to find balance in my life. As when I realized I wanted to listen to audio on my phone the night I watched *Saturday Night Fever*, I started to realize I was becoming anxious if I forgot my phone downstairs while I was upstairs getting ready for work. Sometimes, I would stop myself from going to get the phone solely because I was running late for work. But I came to realize I was getting anxious because of the void, the silence. Purposefully practicing silence during my meditation each day has helped with this anxiety.

I still love listening to personal and professional development audio because I have this immense desire to continuously learn and improve myself. I truly believe setting goals and actively aiming to achieve them is critical for giving our lives meaning, purpose, and direction. But I also believe we can't wait to be happy and enjoy our lives until we reach our goals. We must enjoy the journey along the way. Meditation helped me find joy in my journey.

Meditation is the perfect practice for staying present and maintaining a strong focus. Practicing meditation created a sense of calm and happiness within me. Often, people who've been traumatized are in a constant state of hyperarousal, so they need ways to help them relax and feel safe. To this end, meditation has been very beneficial for me. It brings me a sense of calm, quiets my mind, and relieves tension in my body.

Whenever you notice that uncomfortable feelings come up, don't ignore them. Acknowledging painful feelings without pushing them away is a critical part of the healing process. Many chronic pain conditions are thought to be associated with holding onto trauma and difficult experiences. Instead of trying to erase difficult feelings, use them as a gentle reminder to yourself. They can remind you to practice self-care in the moment before you get overwhelmed by emotion. Maybe you simply need to sit back, take a deep breath, and focus on grounding. You might notice your feet grounded on the floor or how you're grounded in your seat. Feeling a sense of groundedness keeps you present in the moment and reminds you that you're currently safe, and the only unsettling thing is your thoughts. Maybe you need to stop what you're doing and go for a short walk. When we catch difficult emotions right at the beginning, it doesn't take long to work through them.

Pushing the emotions further and further down creates a sensation of a dam breaking when we're exposed to one final stressor. The emotions just begin to flood out of you. Learning how to acknowledge difficult feelings and be able to work through them with different self-care techniques is essential to healing from trauma. Because trauma affects our capacity to cope, we move through trauma by relearning how to cope. Self-care is critical in this process.

You can use a variety of options when you become flooded with emotions as well as options to prevent that flooding from occurring in the first place. Meditation is one of those options. Depending on how long I'm meditating for and what I feel would serve me the most that day, I do one of the following meditations or a combination of a few of them.

In the coming sections, I'll describe some of my favorite forms of meditation, why I like them, and instructions on how to try each of them yourself. For each of the meditations I discuss, you'll want to start in a comfortable seated position. You can use props like a pillow, bolster, or rolled blanket to sit on. You might be more comfortable if you sit on something that allows your hips to be level with or higher than your knees. This decreases the likelihood your feet will fall asleep if you're sitting cross-legged. You can also use props, like yoga blocks or rolled towels/blankets, to put under each knee when in a cross-legged position.

Sitting on a prop makes it easier to sit with your spine erect longer. If sitting on the floor without back support isn't comfortable, you can sit up against a wall for support. You can even place a support behind your back. If that's still too uncomfortable, you can sit in a chair. I don't recommend that you lie down because you'll more likely fall asleep during the meditation. However, if that's the only position that works for you, then go for it. Being in pain makes it harder to concentrate on your meditation. Mild discomfort might be impossible to avoid if you suffer from chronic pain, so gauge for yourself what level of discomfort you can handle while still being able to focus during the meditation. Personally, I suffer from chronic back and knee pain, so it's difficult for me to get comfortable during meditation. I always aim to get myself into a position where I won't fall asleep and can stay there for 10 to 15 minutes at a time.

The amount of time you spend meditating will vary greatly based on several factors. I don't recommend jumping right into a 30-minute meditation if you've never done it. I think 5 minutes is a good number to start with. Again, adjust your practice as you need. If 5 minutes is extremely difficult, then move it down to 2 minutes and slowly increase it as you feel comfortable. When 5 minutes becomes easy, then move it up to 7 or 10 minutes, then 15 minutes. What's most important is setting yourself up for success. Many people, especially those who've been traumatized, get very anxious when alone with their thoughts. So, don't worry if you have to take it slow. Even one minute is beneficial. We're surrounded by so much noise from people, televisions, phones, and the radio that we rarely have silence in our lives. Some of it may very well be self-imposed to purposely avoid being alone with your thoughts. If troubling thoughts arise while you're meditating, take a deep breath, remind yourself you're safe right now, and return to your point of focus in the meditation. It's empowering to know that troubling thoughts can arise and you can consciously choose to let them go.

It's important to learn how to sit with pain and discomfort until it passes. This is one reason why meditation is so helpful. Meditation teaches us how to let go of the intrusive thoughts that are constantly seeping in from all sides. It allows you to let distressing thoughts or feelings come in, acknowledge them, refocus on your breath, and let the thoughts dissipate.

In the beginning, if sitting in silence is overwhelming, try a guided meditation. Guided meditations are often helpful to those who are meditating for the first time or learning a new type of meditation. You can find lots of examples of guided meditations on YouTube and apps on your phone like Insight Timer. I also like to use Insight Timer to time my meditations and provide me with signals when it's time to transition to a new stage of my meditation. Over time, you'll be able to do each meditation without any guidance.

## Three-Part Breath

The three-part breath is something I teach all my students, whether it's in a college classroom, my coaching clients, or a group I'm speaking to about self-care. The three-part breath is one of the quickest ways to calm yourself down and ease stress and anxiety.

This kind of meditation is extremely portable, so you can do it anywhere: during an exam, in the bathroom, in bed, or in line at the grocery store. It also allows you to draw your focus back to your breath if you get distracted and your mind starts to wander.

Understanding the basics of breathwork is so powerful because it gives us a foundation for how and why meditation affects the body. Our sympathetic nervous system, what people refer to as our fight-or-flight response, causes us to take more frequent, shallow breaths from our chest. Whereas, our parasympathetic nervous system, our rest-and-digest system, causes us to take less frequent, deeper belly breaths.

If you notice a baby breathing, their belly will expand on each in-breath. Whereas, when you watch most adults breathe, their belly comes in and their chest expands on each in-breath, which is why they're referred to as "chest breathers." As Lee Albert points out in *Yoga for Pain Relief*, chest breathers are only filling the upper third of their lungs with oxygen with every breath. This means that they're only taking in 30% to 40% of the oxygen that they could be.[6] They also aren't fully expelling the carbon dioxide, a waste product, from their lungs.

Therefore, deeper belly breaths, allow you to maximize your oxygen intake and release the maximum amount of waste from your lungs. In addition, if you force yourself to breathe out of your belly, you're signaling to your brain that you're okay. If you can focus on consciously breathing into your belly, that must mean you're not in danger and the sympathetic nervous system will calm down. At that point, your heart rate and breathing rate can begin to slow, and the tension in your muscles will begin to subside.

Beth, a friend of mine, told me that she purposely held her breath as she heard her perpetrator coming. She would hide in the closet and would try not to make a sound, hoping that he wouldn't find her. She said she started to hold her breath or breathe very shallow anytime she heard him move around the house. For my friend, taking shallow breaths was a way to try to protect herself from another late-night visit from her victimizer. But this habit of shallow breathing followed her from childhood into late adulthood. If you're like Beth, focusing on deep breathing can help retrain your body and mind to let it know that it's okay to take deep breaths.

Breathing into your belly even has added benefits of helping to get things moving in your digestive tract. So, if you have problems with constipation, this is a terrific exercise to do regularly. Stress can take a toll on our digestive tract, and one way to relieve that is through breathing exercises, like the three-part breath.

When I'm either by myself or in yoga class doing this

meditation, I like to place one hand on my belly and one hand on my heart. I can feel the slight separation of my hands on the inhale and how they come closer together on the exhale.

One style of doing this is to place your hands over your heart and think of moments for which you're grateful. When I was doing this at a workshop, we were asked to pull in moments we were proud of and achievements that made us feel strong and whole. I focused on the beautiful places I've seen and the experiences I've had. This experience was so powerful for me. I held onto my heart and was filled with gratitude for the beat of my heart. It made me remember how many times I wanted to take my own life, how my life has changed so much, and everything I would have missed out on if I had taken my own life. I became filled with immense gratitude that my heart was still beating. As I stood there with my hands on my heart, tears started to stream down my face. To this day, I put my hand on my heart whenever I need a shot of gratitude. What made the experience even more powerful was discussing what came up for us during the activity. One of the guys in my group gave me a big hug and just held on. It's why these types of events are so powerful. They bring together a community of people with similar life circumstances and the desire to improve their lives. It's powerful to know that no matter how hard things have been, the suffering can end, and if others have made it through their own battles, you can too.

I truly feel meditation helps you with being able to identify more things for which you're grateful. With the perpetual chatter we have going on inside our minds, it's hard to see through it all and focus on the good around us. As Tony Robbins says, "Where focus goes, energy flows."

Although some forms of meditation encourage keeping the eyes open with a soft gaze on one point, I prefer to meditate with my eyes closed. It allows me to be more in touch with what's happening in my body. With my eyes open, I focus more on the external environment but with my eyes closed, I focus more on what I'm feeling inside.

However, closing your eyes during meditation may be uncomfortable if you don't feel safe in the current space. It's okay to keep your eyes open with a soft gaze if that makes you more comfortable. However, I encourage you to find a place to meditate where you feel safe. When you feel safe, you're able to fully relax, which allows you to reap the full benefits of meditation. But don't get discouraged if it's difficult in the beginning. Being uncomfortable with silence is natural, even if we haven't been traumatized. So be patient with yourself. Give yourself time to practice and remember to start out small.

Try not to get discouraged with your practice if it takes a while to work up to longer periods of silence. Meditation is called a practice for a reason. It takes time to get comfortable and make it part of your routine. Every person's path through healing from trauma is going to be different. What works for one person, may not work for another. Take time to explore what works for you and don't dismiss something outright if it doesn't work the first time. It's about practicing patience with yourself and the tool that you're using. By taking time, you're being kind to yourself and giving yourself the opportunity to learn and grow and really find what works best for you.

## Try It Yourself: The Three-Part Breath

- Get yourself into a comfortable seated position.
- Gently close your eyes or keep a soft gaze down toward the floor. Relax your face and body, close your mouth, and breathe naturally through your nose.
- Observe the natural inhalation and exhalation of your breath but don't change anything. Just focus on the inhale and exhale. If you become distracted by other thoughts, just notice them, and then let them go. Then focus your attention back to the inhales and the exhales.
- Place one or both hands on your belly.
- Begin to focus your awareness on your breath as it moves in and out of your body and deeply inhale through your nose.
- Expand your belly with each breath like a balloon inflating with air.
- Exhale through your nose while drawing your navel back toward your spine. Completely empty your belly of air.
- Repeat this process for five breaths.
- Move one or both hands a little higher and place on the bottom of your ribs.
- On the next breath, fill your belly full of air and then take in a little bit more air as you expand the rib cage.
- As you exhale, release the air from your rib cage first and then your belly.
- Repeat for five breaths.
- Place one or both hands on your chest, right below your collar bones.

- On the next breath, fill your belly and rib cage full of air and then take in a little bit more air into your upper chest causing the area where your heart is to rise.
- As you exhale, release the breath from your upper chest, then your rib cage, and finally your belly.
- Continue as you feel comfortable for 10 more breaths.

If progressing to breathing into your rib cage or upper chest causes you to strain to breathe, you can stay with belly breathing and progress over time. In the beginning, it can be difficult to breathe into the rib cage and upper chest, but don't get discouraged. In fact, some people feel uncomfortable and scared during the strain of inhaling for such a long time. As you practice the three-part breath, you'll find that these feelings subside. For now, meet your body where it is currently, and don't force yourself to do anything you aren't ready for.

You can stop with the three phases of breathing or add another level.
- Imagine bringing in what would serve you with each inhale. Maybe that's patience, love, compassion, relief, or strength.
- Sense it filling you up with each deep inhale.
- As you breathe, inhale what will serve you, then exhale anything that's not serving you or what may be holding you back in some way: physical pain, emotional pain, or sadness.

Signs of stress show up in the body before the mind is consciously aware we're under stress. How does stress show up in your body? Does your heart beat faster? Does your face get hot? Does your chest feel tight? Do you feel tension build in your muscles? Do you feel a knot in your stomach? Noticing the signs of stress early can cut it off at the pass before your stress rises to extreme levels. Next time you notice any signs of stress showing up, use this three-part breathing technique.

During my years as a college professor, I taught a variety of courses on human anatomy and physiology, including neurobiology. I'm fascinated by how our brain develops and how it responds to extreme stress. During childhood and early adolescence, we depend largely on a primitive, emotional part of our brain called the amygdala for decision making and problem solving. As we progress through adolescence, the role of decision making and problem solving begins to be taken over by the prefrontal cortex, which allows for rational decision making. However, under extreme stress, even as adults, communication with our prefrontal cortex gets temporarily cut off and the amygdala begins to take over. Some of the many functions of the amygdala include processing fearful and threatening stimuli and activating the fight or flight response. That's why we should never say things when we're really upset. We should walk away and calm down so we can think more clearly. Having a technique like stepping away before you say something you might regret or focusing on breathing in place to deal with a situation in front of you with ease, can create a space for you to think more clearly.

Meditation is just one of the many tools and techniques you can use when you feel overwhelmed or out of control. It helps you to feel in control of your mind, body, and, ultimately, your life. Learning to control your breath is one of the single most important things you can do to start taking back control of your life. It proves you have control over something. Once you learn to focus on your breath and practice meditating, you'll start to learn that you have control over so much more than just your breath.

Meditation can be very challenging for those just starting out, especially for those who've experienced trauma. The silence can be overwhelming. But learning to be quiet and still will change your life because it shows you that as disturbing thoughts come into your mind, you can let them go by drawing your attention back to your point of focus. Meditation is great for helping you to focus and not allowing the constant chatter inside and outside of your mind derail you off your path. Meditation, especially breathing exercises like the three-part breath, show that you have the power to quickly change how you're feeling. This means that you're not helpless or hopeless.

## Mindfulness Meditation

Mindfulness meditation helps you to become present. It's great for helping you recognize your ability to redirect your own thoughts. You're in control. You can let memories or thoughts come in that are troubling and just let them pass, like everything does in life.

It's very empowering to know you can let uncomfortable feelings arise and then let them go. Dealing with negative emotions when they're not so strong will prevent them from reaching an overwhelming state. Most people do their best to avoid negative emotions altogether because they're painful and uncomfortable, but bottling everything up and not letting it go creates its own set of problems. When I was younger, I just blocked everything out. I bottled it up and pretended it didn't happen so I could go on with my life. Because of this, I've been struggling with chronic pain since my early twenties. Although I still experience them from time-to-time, I used to be very prone to crying at every little bit of stress at work or at home. I would cry or go off the handle and yell and scream. The chronic pain and crying fits have largely been caused by me holding everything inside.

I have found that as I practice sitting with negative and uncomfortable feelings, breathing deeply, acknowledging the thoughts, and letting them go, I'm not as wildly emotional as I was before. I still get upset and teary-eyed, but I don't notice as many extremes as I used to. My therapists have each wondered if I'm bipolar. But they never formally assigned me a bipolar diagnosis because they felt it's how I've coped with my traumas over time. Now I can control my emotional extremes through different coping mechanisms.

Mindfulness meditation is helpful in refocusing the mind. By redirecting your mind to come back to an area of focus during meditation, like your breath, when your mind wanders during meditation, you're training it for the distractions you're constantly being bombarded with each day. If we're at home and our significant other or our child is trying to have a conversation with us, but our mind keeps wandering to the project that's overdue at work, this practice trains our mind to bring our attention back to our loved one. If we're at work and our mind wanders on something not work related, practicing mindfulness trains our mind to refocus on work. In my case, I had to train my mind to come back to the present and learn to feel positive emotions again.

## *Try It Yourself: Mindfulness Meditation*

Settle into a comfortable seated position. Close your eyes. Bring your attention to your surrounding environment. What sounds do you hear? Listen. Start with the sounds closest to you and move your attention outwards.

Bring your attention to physical sensations: the temperature of the air on your skin, the clothing on your skin. Notice where you are grounded in your seat.

Bring your attention to the air in your nostrils. Notice the temperature. What do you smell? Start by becoming aware of your breath. Feel your breath come into your abdomen. Focus on your belly expanding with each inhale and coming in with each exhale.

Notice any sensations in your body. Where do you feel tension or discomfort? Breathe into that area and visualize the tension slowly being released by your body with each exhale.

Without judgment, focus on your current feelings and emotions. If you find yourself going down the rabbit hole, refocus on your breath without criticizing yourself for thinking troubling thoughts.

When ready, take a deep inhale, then exhale, and slowly open your eyes.

Mindfulness can be practiced anywhere with eyes open, not just during meditation. And it can be practiced in all different aspects of your life. It's simply a practice of staying present in the moment. You can practice mindfulness by really listening to the person you're talking with in the moment. If you're walking, it's about noticing all the different sensations you're experiencing from the environment around you: the wind, the temperature, sights, smells, and sounds.

After being traumatized, it's common to ruminate over the past, what you've lost, and what will no longer be. You continue to spin your wheels, but you aren't moving. This vicious cycle, looping through the past, needs to be broken. People who are overcoming trauma need to learn how to distinguish between what was then and what's happening now. Just because something happened in the past, doesn't mean it will happen again in the future. The fear of being hurt again can paralyze people and prevent them from acting. It starts to become cemented in their mind that their trauma has forever altered the course of their life in a terrible way, and nothing will ever change their course. Focusing on the present with a mindfulness meditation opens the mind to the possibility of moving forward and living in the moment, which also changes the course of their life.

## Loving-Kindness Meditation

I love the loving-kindness meditation because it cultivates a feeling of love and compassion that I carry far beyond the time that I'm meditating. It allows me to release judgment and hostility toward myself and others. It allows me to feel love for those who cause me pain because I know they're also in pain. Those who inflict the most pain on others are likely in the most need of love. This can be a very difficult pill to swallow, especially for those of us who've been violated by another person. Please know I'm not trying to justify any wrong one person does to another. What I do know, however, is that by carrying around pain from our traumas, we revictimize ourselves over and over with our own thoughts, sometimes long after our perpetrators are dead and gone. By being able to cultivate love for all beings, including yourself, a weight can start to be lifted from you. It was fascinating for me the first time it really hit me that each of the men who violated me were likely violated themselves either sexually, physically, or emotionally. Then I saw forgiveness might be possible when previously, I thought forgiveness would never be in reach.

Please know how much I understand that the concept of forgiveness can seem absurd, given what we've endured. I went through a period of my life when I was trying to think of ways I could go around murdering all rapists without getting caught. I imagined being a vigilante, saving all those who weren't being saved by anyone else. I would be the one to end their suffering. I would be the one to prevent the future suffering of others by killing these soul suckers. What's interesting, though, is that by starting to cultivate forgiveness for my abusers, I began to see they're that way because they already felt dead inside. It made me start to realize there actually needs to be a place for perpetrators to heal.

It was an amazing experience to be at a book reading at Spoken Interludes in Hastings-On-Hudson, where I had the privilege and honor of sitting right in front of Eve Ensler as she read part of her book, *The Apology*. She opened the room up for questions once she was done reading and I asked her a question about whether we should have ways for victimizers to apologize and work through their own pain. She said that we do need to create safe spaces for them, and we can do that by creating small groups within our communities.[7]

When you reach the part of the loving-kindness meditation when you focus on a difficult person in your life, you don't have to go right to the person who has caused you the most pain in your life. Eventually, you can work up to that. But if that thought is triggering for you, then start out with someone who won't be as difficult for you to send love and kindness to and work up to the most difficult people in your life, past or present. If the difficult person you initially pick becomes too challenging, you can simply pick a different difficult person in your life who's easier to send love and kindness to. Or you can go back to someone whom you love and work up to sending love and kindness to a difficult person as you continue to practice this meditation.

By cultivating a deep sense of love, this meditation is also very important to help strengthen your current relationships and your compassion for strangers. Most importantly, this meditation will help strengthen self-love and self-acceptance. At 12, one of my victimizers told me that I was so disgusting, I should be thankful anyone even wanted to touch my body. My self-loathing began to spiral out of control after that, leading me to exercise vigorously to lose weight. It then transitioned into me binging and purging. At my worst, I was purging up to 12 times a day. I also became hypersexualized, as I tried to get approval from men that I wasn't disgusting anymore.

I never thought I could truly love myself. Through all the methods provided in this book, I've finally begun to love myself and accept my flaws. I still struggle with it some days, but so many things I previously thought were impossible have become possible.

## *Try It Yourself: Loving-Kindness Meditation*

Sit in a comfortable position. Gently close your eyes or keep them open with a soft gaze toward the floor. Draw your attention toward your breath. Take two or three slow, deep breaths. Inhale deeply through your nose and release a cleansing exhale through your mouth. Lengthen the exhale and fully empty the lungs with each exhale. Let your breath return to normal. Close your mouth and breath only through your nose. Focus on the movement of your chest and abdomen as you inhale and exhale. Notice your heart beating. You can place one or both hands on your chest to help feel your heartbeat.

Maintaining your focus on your heartbeat, think about all that you have to be grateful for. It might be your health, your family, your career, your home, and it might be a combination of many things. Then bring your attention back to your heartbeat. It might help to place your hand on your heart. Notice how you feel.

Begin to cultivate the love you have for yourself. If this becomes difficult, think of how you would feel if you truly loved yourself the way you hope for. Sending loving-kindness to yourself, repeat each phrase three to four times silently or vocally depending on your location. If you're in a group, you can say them silently or softly; if you're on a mountaintop, you can shout them out:

May I be happy.

May I be healthy.

May I be safe.

May I be at peace.

Once you feel love filling your heart, bring your attention back to your heartbeat and notice how you feel. Did your thoughts or sensations in your body change?

Think of a person whom you love. It might be a family member, a friend, teacher, or a pet. Pick a person or pet who loves you unconditionally without expecting anything in return. Send loving-kindness to that person, repeat each phrase three to four times silently or out loud:

May you be happy.

May you be healthy.

May you be safe.

May you be at peace.

Once you feel love filling your heart, bring your attention back to your heartbeat and notice how you feel.

Think of a neutral person or stranger. It might be someone at work you've never spoken to or the cashier at your grocery store. Send loving-kindness to that person, repeat each phrase three to four times silently or out loud:

May you be happy.

May you be healthy.

May you be safe.

May you be at peace.

Once you feel love filling your heart, bring your attention back to your heartbeat and notice how you feel.

Think of a person you're having difficulty with or had

difficulty with and is no longer in your life. Try not to get caught up with the anger or frustration you may have toward them. Instead, focus on the fact that they're a person who has flaws and has experienced suffering. Sending loving-kindness to that person, repeat each phrase three to four times silently or out loud:

May you be happy.

May you be healthy.

May you be safe.

May you be at peace.

Don't worry if this is difficult for you. Bring your attention back to your heartbeat and notice how you feel.

Think about all beings on this Earth, human and nonhuman. Feel how connected we all are, people, animals, plants, and all other living beings. Sending loving-kindness to all beings, repeat each phrase three to four times silently or out loud:

May all beings be happy.

May all beings be healthy.

May all beings be safe.

May all beings be at peace.

Once you feel love filling your heart, bring your attention back to your heartbeat and notice how you feel. Bring your awareness to the movement of your chest and abdomen as you inhale and exhale. Slowly open your eyes. Slowly bring movement back into your body. Maybe move around your hands and feet and stretch out your legs.

Please feel free to alter these messages to more accurately reflect the love and kindness you want to send out to the world. You can also alter the length of time of the meditation by focusing on more than one individual during each stage of the meditation. You can also add more layers to who you're sending your love and kindness out to. When I'm doing a longer meditation, after I send out love and kindness to a neutral person or stranger, I then send love and kindness to everyone at my job, then I move out to everyone in the Capital Region in New York, then out to all of New York, then out to all the U.S., and then out to the whole world. You can focus on your heartbeat or breath for as long as you would like. You benefit from the meditation regardless of how many layers you go down into it. Just know it can be as long or as short as you want to make it.

This meditation can be practiced in any posture, not just a seated cross-legged position. It can be practiced throughout your day when you're at home, at work, in the grocery store, or walking down the sidewalk. When I see someone in pain or discomfort, I inhale deeply and say the four phases in my head:

May you be happy.

May you be healthy.

May you be safe.

May you be at peace.


I immediately soften and begin to feel true love and compassion for them as a living being who deserves love, joy, and happiness.

# Tonglen Meditation

Although I find all these forms of meditation to be powerful, Tonglen meditation is one of my favorites. I first learned about this type of meditation from Pema Chödrön's book, *The Places That Scare You*. With each inhale we take in the pain and discomfort from others and with each exhale we send them relief.[8] It's extremely easy to become absorbed by our own pain, especially when we've been traumatized. This meditation draws your attention away from yourself and focuses it onto others. Tonglen meditation increases my sense of empathy toward others. I become more cognizant of the suffering of others. It has also allowed me to see I'm not alone in this world, as I've often felt.

This meditation may not be accessible to you just yet, and that's okay. You may not feel as though you can bring relief to the suffering of others until you've figured out how to end your own suffering. I didn't discover this meditation until I was already in a good place, so I don't know how I would have responded to this meditation when I was in the earlier stages of my grief. I do know, however, that even when I was an adolescent, when my traumas were at their worst, I had an immense desire to help others. I think most people who've been violated in some way have a desire to right the injustices perpetrated against them. Over time I've found that many of my students chose to pursue helping professions because of their own personal life circumstances or because of the circumstances of someone they love.

That's why part of me feels I would have gravitated toward this meditation sooner if I had known about it. It might have made me feel more powerful and in control of what I felt if I could ease someone else's suffering. If I could do that, then maybe there's hope for me to end my own suffering. I encourage you to try it, but if, at any point, you feel overwhelmed, simply stop. You can come back to it in a few hours, days, or years if you feel this meditation could hurt you more than heal you. But I want to introduce you to it in case you think it could help you too.

There are much longer versions of this meditation than what I describe below. Because I mostly use this meditation on the spot, when I'm in the presence of someone in pain and in need of relief, I made the practice below short and simple. By decreasing the length, it becomes a portable tool you can apply anytime and anywhere in your daily life.

## Try It Yourself: Tonglen Meditation

Sit in a comfortable position. Gently close your eyes or keep them open with a soft gaze toward the floor. Draw your attention toward your breath. Take two or three slow, deep breaths. Inhale deeply through your nose and release a cleansing exhale through your mouth. Lengthen the exhale and fully empty the lungs with each exhale. Let your breath return to normal. Close your mouth and breath only through your nose. Focus on the movement of your chest and abdomen as you inhale and exhale.

Bring to your awareness someone you want to help. Imagine you're breathing in their pain. It might be someone who's ill, a person who has recently suffered a loss, anyone who could benefit by a sense of relief. Visualize their pain coming in through every pore of your body. Don't be afraid to do this. Their pain won't become your own. You're doing it so you can feel the love, compassion, and empathy they need to help them feel at peace.

Breathe in as though you're removing their pain from their body with your every inhale. This will create room inside of them to receive the comfort and healing you'll be sending them.

As you exhale, imagine you're sending them all the beauty, joy, and love you have to offer. Please know you're not making these feelings unavailable to yourself by giving them away. Generating love and compassion to send out to others allows us to create more of it inside of us. Visualize yourself having a bottomless well of empathy and compassion to send to that person.

You can continue focusing on that one person, or you can choose to move it out further to all people in the world who suffer from the same circumstances. With each inbreath, you breathe in all their pain and discomfort, and with each outbreath, you send them relief.

Repeat for as long as you would like. Once complete, bring your awareness back to your own breath. Notice how you feel. Do you feel differently than when you began? Take a moment to focus on the difference the practice made to your overall sense of well-being. When ready, take a deep inhale, then exhale and slowly open your eyes.

Like with the loving-kindness meditation, I practice Tonglen meditation when I'm out and about. I'm triggered to complete this meditation whenever I'm in the presence of someone who appears to need relief. Even when I'm driving or walking down the street. It's amazing to see how just spending a few seconds focusing on the pain of others and sending them relief can almost instantly change your emotional state of being. It's a very powerful meditation. I feel that a major benefit to meditation is that it teaches you to be present in the current moment by concentrating on one thing. When you're in the presence of a person who's in pain and draw your attention to them, you're remaining in the present moment. You can focus on removing their pain with a deep inhale and sending them relief with a deep exhale. With that one breath cycle, you can capture a present moment that likely would have passed you by if you were focusing on how much work you have to do, a past trauma, or anxiety over a situation that hasn't even occurred yet.

I've become extremely sensitive to signs of inner stress and turmoil in people, even strangers. I know from experience how easy it is to camouflage pain with a smile. So, it has become easy for me to pick up on when someone else is in pain, whether it be physical or emotional.

In the aftermath of trauma, it's easy to feel isolated. I can remember anger filling me up as I thought of all the traumas I have suffered and not understanding why I had to endure so much pain. I felt like no one understood me and my pain. It's why I gravitated toward men who were in obvious pain, who were also self-destructing, because they would understand. They wouldn't think there was something wrong with me. But starting to notice other people are suffering too helps you see you aren't alone. You don't have to navigate this harsh world all on your own.

By practicing Tonglen, you'll realize you have resources to give away. You'll also see that by giving your resources away you're not diminishing your own store of resources. You still have plenty to give. For a while, I didn't want to be around people because I felt they would drain me of the few resources I felt I had left. But, in reality, spending time with and serving others filled my cup, so I had more resources for myself and others. What I'm hoping you'll notice by taking in the pain of others is that it will fill your heart with compassion toward yourself and others. You'll start to see that many of us are shouldering pain that's weighing us down. This can change how you respond to others and in turn, how others respond to you.

## The Power of Meditation

Meditation is one the most important things you can do to improve your life and help you through your healing journey. I also think it can be one of the hardest. When we experience trauma, we often want to avoid being in silence. We avoid being still. We're scared that scenes from our past will come up and we won't know how to handle it. But that's exactly the reason why meditation is so powerful. It proves to us that painful thoughts can arise and we have the power to let them go. It allows us to stay present and know that was then and this is now.

I didn't start regularly practicing meditation until my mid-30s. I was introduced to it at different points in my life and I can remember saying each time, "I'm not good at meditating." Maybe at those times I wasn't ready to receive the benefits. Keep in mind that you can try many different tools to work through your trauma on your own, and some tools may not be useful at this point in your life and may never be. But in the future, one might be, so I encourage you to keep these different tools in your back pocket as options.

Life is about stages and progression through those stages. What might be useful to you now, may or may not be useful to you throughout the rest of your life. You have to be willing to be flexible and welcoming of new experiences and opportunities. I understand that once traumatized, it's common to become rigid and inflexible. I'm still very rigid and inflexible in many aspects of my life today. This natural response protects us. Rigidity and inflexibility keep us safe. They create order amidst all the chaos going on inside and around us. Rigidity can be an important safety mechanism. But we must know when it's okay to start letting down our guard. Sometimes, we get into a rigid pattern and we're not willing to accept alternatives.

The first thing you try may make it easier for you to try the next. Although I find meditation to be one of the most powerful things we can do to heal, it's not the easiest to implement in the early stages of your healing journey. You can try it and work into it little by little. But if you find it difficult, it may be important to incorporate one of the other tools first and then come back to meditation. Don't be hard on yourself. Remember to start small. If you need to, start with one minute of meditation, then work up to two minutes, then three minutes, and so on. Your path of healing is just a journey, like life, and we need to embrace as many of the bumps and beauty as possible along the way.

Don't condemn yourself for not moving quicker through your grief. Society gives us, and we give ourselves, a timeline for our healing. I cringe every time a client tells me they think or someone else told them that they should be over what happened by now. Who can say you should be healed in six months, one year, or two years, that after a specified period, your trauma should never affect you again? Are those boundaries, those timelines, rooted in reality? And are those timelines the same for everyone? If it takes one person six months to "move on" after a trauma, does that mean everyone should be "over it" within six months? No! There are so many factors that go into determining how long it will take for a person to regain their ability to cope after trauma. How were you traumatized? How old were you when the trauma occurred? Did the trauma occur at the hands of someone you were supposed to trust? Did the trauma occur once or repeatedly over years? Did you experience multiple forms of trauma at different stages of your life? What support mechanisms did you have in place before and after the trauma? All these things will affect a person's ability to cope with trauma and their healing timeline. So please, be kind to yourself and be patient with your own healing journey.

# Chapter 4

# Exercise

Muscles all over my body are constantly tight and sore. My body is continuously reliving my traumas and is always preparing itself for the next attack. Like so many others who've experienced trauma, I try to push the memories from my mind, but they remain anchored in my body. It's why the work of trauma researchers like Dr. Bessel van der Kolk, Dr. Peter Levine, and Dr. James Gordon are so important. They've researched how experiencing trauma makes it difficult to feel safe in your body and have developed ways of helping people to overcome that challenge.

I've also often felt disconnected from my body. I often get hurt when exercising because I have difficulty sensing when I'm pushing my body too far. Although I regularly hurt myself during exercise, even today, it continues to be one of my greatest outlets. I've used exercise throughout most of my healing journey. I would walk and ride my bike for miles as a teenager. I also played sports in middle school and high school. In my early college years, I would run and exercise extensively in the gym. And in my 30s, I took up hiking and yoga.

I also find that I tend to work myself harder when I'm in a group than if I do it by myself. This has pros and cons to it. I burn more calories when I'm in a group. This is even true when I hike in a group versus solo. Group exercise classes are great for learning different types of exercises and for building a sense of community. But I also find that it's harder for me to listen to the cues my body is trying to tell me when I'm in a group. I get injured more when I do group exercises because I usually end up overdoing it. I encourage you to try different types of group exercise whether it's yoga, Zumba, Orangetheory Fitness (OTF), or any wide variety of group exercise classes out there.

But I encourage you to listen to your body when in the classes. Don't expect that you'll be able to do the full expression of each yoga pose when you're first starting, lifting heavy weights in an OTF class, or be able to keep up with the pace of the Zumba instructor. You should be proud of taking the first step to go to an exercise class. You should create a goal of improving over time rather than being perfect right from the start. If, at any point, you feel you're being asked to push farther than you're comfortable with from a group class instructor, don't be afraid to talk to them about it. If necessary, you can find a different class to go to. There are so many options out there, and each one is different!

Through the trauma healing process, exercise can provide you with the opportunity to explore your body in ways you may have never done before. What feels good? What doesn't? What's your body trying to tell you? What do you need more or less of? Our bodies contain so much wisdom, we just have to learn to listen. Unfortunately, we're trained from an early age to resist what our bodies tell us. We hold bowel movements in because we're embarrassed to have them at work. We take pain medications to mask physical pain. We take antidepressants to mask emotional pain. We ingest caffeine to mask our bodies' pleas for us to rest. In each of these instances, our body is telling us one thing, but we're choosing not to listen. Over time, it becomes difficult to listen to and understand the messages that our body is sending to us, because the message is getting garbled by the noise of medication or supplementation.

## Hiking

I never go part way into anything. So, when I started hiking, I got so into it that for a few years in a row, I was hiking at least 135 mountains per year. I'm blessed by living in the Capital District in New York because there are so many mountains available. I have the Catskill Mountains one and a half hours south of me, the Adirondack Mountains two hours North of me, the Berkshire Mountains in Massachusetts one hour East of me, and with a three- or four-hour drive, I also have access to the Green Mountains in Vermont and the White Mountains in New Hampshire.

The mountains served such an important part in my life, specifically in my healing journey. In the mountains, I was able to truly heal my deep wounds. For the first few years, I hiked many of the mountains by myself. With being morbidly obese, I was slow, and I was self-conscious about my pace. I've always been on the clumsy side, so when I hiked with people who were faster than me and I started to get tired, I was more likely to fall or roll an ankle. So, I just learned to enjoy my own company. This turned out to be a blessing for me.

I was asked by a friend who was battling with ending a relationship, "How do you deal with loneliness?" She explained that breaking up is so hard for her because it leads her to making poor decisions. I acknowledged that was also something I used to struggle with a lot. What I eventually realized is that by keeping people in my life or putting people in my life who weren't good for me, just so I had a placeholder while I worked through the breakup, I was actually hurting myself even more. I had to see that I was being hurt more by putting toxic people in my life or leaving them in my life than just from being alone. By starting to force myself to be alone, I started to enjoy my own company. That's when hiking became very powerful for me and why hiking by myself was very important for me. In the mountains, I learned to be okay by myself.

People have always criticized me immensely for hiking by myself. I'm a woman, hiking alone in the woods. They scolded me for not knowing how dangerous it was. People would often say out loud, "Are you nuts?!" Or I could see it in the way they looked at me or how their voice changed. What they don't realize is how therapeutic being in nature by myself has been. They don't realize that when I really came to enjoy being by myself, I stopped putting people in my life just so I wouldn't feel lonely. It changed everything for me.

Yes, I do take precautions. I make sure to always carry a headlamp and pack extra water, food, and gear in case I'm out longer than expected. I've taken many trainings on wilderness safety. I know how to use a map and compass. I do what I can to protect myself. However, one of my favorite personal sayings that I have said for years is, "I can't wait to live my life until I have someone to live it with." We must learn to be self-sufficient. What happens when there's no one around? How do we take care of ourselves? How many stories have you heard of women not knowing what to do after they get divorced or widowed because their husbands took care of everything for them? Yes, there's safety in knowing that someone else is there to help shoulder tasks and burdens associated with daily life, but it's also important to be able to navigate life independently. Divorce and death of a partner can be shattering for people who can no longer clearly distinguish the boundaries between where they and their loved ones begin and end.

I'm not encouraging you to go hiking by yourself, especially if you're inexperienced. But I am encouraging you to find an activity you enjoy doing by yourself so you can learn to enjoy your own company and learn to take care of your own needs. I do feel that having human connections is important. Humans are naturally social creatures. But in the trauma healing process, it's important to learn to trust yourself, your own instincts, and the messages your body is trying to send you. It's easiest to accomplish this when you're by yourself.

If it's not hiking, you can go for walks, jog, or ride a bike. There are indoor activities you can do by yourself, but being outside is very therapeutic, and I encourage you to find time to regularly spend outside by yourself. Breathing in the fresh air, feeling the sun on your skin, listening to the wind move through the trees, and watching the birds gliding through the sky can be rejuvenating.

## Yoga

My joint and muscle pain started to get worse with the constant pounding on my body from hiking. So, I started doing yoga to increase my balance and flexibility with the hope of decreasing the injuries to my joints while hiking. Yoga turned out to be an immense gift in my life. It took my healing to a whole other level. My yoga practice led me to meditation and improving my diet.

Practicing yoga is when I first learned to listen to my body, when I learned that I had control of my body. We often fail to listen to the wisdom our bodies are trying to share with us. There has always been so much in my life that has been out of my control. Yoga has reinforced for me that what I can control is my mind and body. Yoga has literally changed my life. Most people don't realize that it's more than just a physical practice; it's a way of life. It's about being kind to yourself and kind to others. Through yoga, I've learned to stay when I'm experiencing discomfort. When I first started yoga, I would come out of any pose at the first sign of discomfort. But while completing Baron Baptiste's,"40 days to Personal Revolution" program through The Hot Yoga Spot in Albany, New York, we were encouraged to stay through the discomfort. The purpose was to see that all discomfort will end. Nothing lasts forever. It really brought up all the various habits I had acquired over time to help me deal with the discomfort I was in versus staying with the discomfort until it passed.

I really took this to heart. I always considered hiking as a training ground for life. Reaching a summit when I thought I wasn't physically capable of doing so helped me work through different parts of my trauma. Now yoga became my new training ground. I've experienced so many traumas throughout different stages of my life, yet I've been able to complete my PhD, have a great career, and have traveled around the world. I could only accomplish those things because of periods of calm when the storm let up. Yoga trained me to be calm when enduring a storm, so I could fully embrace the times in my life when the storms have passed. And storms *always* pass.

## Try It Yourself: Yoga

You can practice yoga by yourself at home or with a group in a class. If you're new to yoga, be sure to look for a class that's marked as beginner level. At first, I wouldn't recommend an "all-levels" class until you've taken at least a few beginner-level courses. All-levels classes are typically taught at the intermediate level and the instructor provides some modifications either up or down for the pose. Students new to yoga can find "all-levels" courses to be quite intense. Students are also more likely to get hurt because they don't want to feel that they can't handle the more difficult poses. But please remember that you don't have to look like everyone else in the room. You can let your instructor know ahead of time if you don't want to be touched, if you'll be modifying, or if you're a beginner. It may be tempting to give up on yoga if you end up in a class where there are manual assists and adjustments. Instead of giving up, think of how empowering it will be to learn to advocate for yourself. To choose what happens to your body and when.

Be sure to listen to your own body. Feel free to go to the back of the room if being in front is uncomfortable for you. It's okay if you don't look the same as everyone else in the class. If you worry about doing this, you can always talk to the instructor about your concerns before or after the class.

Or you can do yoga at home. You can watch a yoga video on your phone, computer, or TV, or create your own individual practice to do in the privacy of your own home. A group class will likely not target all your individual needs, which is why creating your own personal practice can be helpful.

In the beginning, you'll need ideas of what to do. I highly recommend Lee Albert's book, *Yoga for Pain Relief*, so you can learn how to make your own individual practice that can be altered at different points in time based on your own specific muscular imbalances.

Doing group classes at first can also give you ideas of what poses you would like to do at home in your own private practice. Group classes can provide you with the opportunity to learn which poses serve you and which don't. You can learn which are beyond your current physical level and are, instead, poses to possibly aspire to completing in the future.

Recognize that people who have experienced trauma can become uncomfortable with the silence and stillness during the final resting pose in yoga. It's important to experience the silence. Know that you're not alone in feeling uncomfortable during this final pose, as, believe it or not, this pose is often considered one of the most difficult. You don't need a lot of supplies. Most people start with a mat and a blanket that can be rolled up for support. However, there are blocks and other accessories to purchase if you want. The best part is, you only need a space on the floor, even a yoga mat is optional.

Exercise can show you how much choice you have over your body. You just have to listen to your body and what it's trying to tell you. If you're continuously pushing down and away hard feelings and emotions, it's going to be difficult to filter out the signals that your body is trying to tell you. It's going to be hard to tell the difference between when you're in actual physical pain versus pain from the trauma buried in your body. If we learn to mistrust everyone, including ourselves and our own judgment, it's going to be difficult to start to listen to signals of when we're truly safe and unsafe. Exercise will help you learn to listen to your body; just start slow and know that, each day, you'll make progress toward healing, both physically and mentally.

# Chapter 5

# Mindful Eating

During my teenage years, my eating disorder was at its worst. At times, I was binging and purging 8-12 times per day. It was astonishing how many thousands of calories I would put into my body each day, just to throw them back up. I would also stay up until two or three o'clock in the morning exercising. This was on top of the exercise I would do for the high school sports I was engaged in. I'll never forget the time my mother came into my room one night when I was completing a Tae Bo workout video and asked if I was taking drugs. "Are you on speed?" she asked. How could I be up so late and still have the energy to exercise? What she didn't understand was just how purely disgusted I was by my body. Because of this, I needed to do whatever I could to rid myself of the current body I was in.

Even though two decades have passed since then, I still struggle with these same thoughts. I haven't purged in a few years, which is why my bulimia is considered to be in remission. But I still binge or eat until my stomach hurts from time-to-time. My greatest power struggle is with food. It's my one great love and my preferred form of self-destruction. Food has always been my go-to pseudo-remedy to relieve any kind of uncomfortable feelings. I use food to celebrate and to push away difficult thoughts, feelings, and emotions.

Like many of my family members, I've struggled with weight for my entire life. I've always had an unhealthy relationship with food. I reached my lowest weight at my adult height of 5 feet and 4 inches tall during my senior year in high school at 118 pounds when my eating disorder was at its worst. I reached my heaviest recorded weight of 222 pounds 10 years later at the age of 28. I likely weighed more than that at one point, but I avoided weighing myself for a few years after Stan died. That's when my weight started piling on so quickly that stretch marks started to sprout up on my stomach as if I were pregnant.

Mindful eating has been one of the most important factors in working through my eating disorder. Mindful eating encouraged me to evaluate the emotions driving my desire to eat. It also encourages me to focus on my food, its textures, and sensations so I don't overeat and give my body time to send me signals that I'm full. I still have more work to do, but I've made a lot of healthy progress from the practice of mindful eating.

I've always tried to fill my days with as much as possible, as I'm always trying to accomplish something. What I've begun to realize is that by always being busy, I don't have time to confront what I'm feeling. I would even fill the time when I was eating with listening to TV, music, or audiobooks so I wouldn't have to be alone with my thoughts.

As I started to practice mindful eating, I realized most of the time I ate or wanted to eat, especially something unhealthy, wasn't when I was hungry, but when I was trying to avoid uncomfortable thoughts or feelings swirling around my mind. That's why when I tried eating in silence at the Omega Institute and then at Kripalu, I was first astonished by how uncomfortable it was. I've always been uncomfortable with silence. But after I worked through the discomfort of the silence, I realized by eating in silence, I could focus on what I was eating and the signals my body was trying to send me.

Now I have my students practice mindful eating as an assignment in the nutrition course I teach at a local community college. Two months after completing the assignment, one of my students emailed me that she had lost 17 pounds by practicing mindful eating!

## Try It Yourself: Mindful Eating

When you sit down to your next meal, before you take your first bite, stop for a moment, and evaluate: How do you feel right now? What made you sit down to eat? Were you hungry, bored, or anxious?

Once you start eating, try this exercise. Take a bite of food, place your fork, knife, or spoon down, rest your hands down on your lap and close your eyes while you chew. You may never have realized that you must contract muscles in your arms and hands to hold your arm up and grasp your fork. So, you're expending energy and focus on that rather than the food you're consuming. Closing your eyes and relaxing your arms down will help you to focus on what you're eating - the textures, tastes, and temperature of the food. It will also allow you to focus on how you're feeling while you're eating. Stopping and relaxing your body while eating will help you not get distracted from the experience.

Then try eating with your non-dominant hand. This requires more focused attention. You'll likely eat more slowly and feel full sooner than if you were to eat more quickly.

After you finish your meal, ask yourself the following questions: How did you know to stop eating? Did you keep eating even after you felt satisfied? Did you continue to eat even after you felt too full? If you kept eating, why? Did you not want to waste food? Just because?

If you did overeat, this isn't about judging your choices. It's about becoming aware of when you do it and why. When you increase your awareness, you'll be able to change your eating habits.

Although it would be immensely beneficial to practice mindful eating for every meal, I know that can seem overwhelming. If it doesn't seem possible for you to do throughout the whole meal, then start small. People tend to give up on goals and making changes when they fail to chunk their goals down into bite-sized pieces. Maybe you start with one meal and modify one thing. You could start with recognizing why you're eating in the first place. Then consider taking away any distractions while you're eating: no talking, phone, TV, book, or newspaper. If this is hard, take some time to think about why it's difficult for you. It's important to understand why you don't want to do something. If it's the silence, try experiencing it. I know after experiencing trauma, silence can be quite uncomfortable. Just as with meditation, notice that by focusing your attention, in this case on what you're eating, you're able to acknowledge a troubling thought, and go back to focusing on what you're eating. With practice, you'll become empowered by your ability to allow disruptive thoughts to come in but not trigger you.

I noticed from practicing mindful eating while traveling or at some type of gathering that if I think I might not get to experience the same thing again, I typically end up overeating or at least want to overeat. I usually eat way too fast, but I notice I eat even faster when I think the food is limited or if I think I won't have the opportunity to experience it again. It's all based out of a scarcity mindset and FOMO, the fear of missing out. I try to remind myself that this is even more reason to savor what I'm eating. We only ever have this one moment.

## A Note on Intermittent Fasting

Another practice that has helped me to learn how to listen to the signals my body is sending is intermittent fasting. My recorded highest weight was 222 lbs. By Spring 2018 I had gotten down to 145 lbs. However, by 2019, I had gotten back up to the 160s and wavered between 160 and 165 for over a year. In September 2020, I started intermittent fasting consistently and got my weight down to 146 by April 2021. I fast for 16-18 hours per day and have little issue with hunger because I've reached appetite correction due to my hunger and satiety hormones having been brought back into balance.

I started intermittent fasting to make a lasting change in my weight. It was a great practice for me to learn what hunger felt like.

Since I was always using food to avoid difficult thoughts, I forgot what actual hunger felt like. It's essential to understand that hunger and appetite are two very different concepts. Hunger is physiological and occurs when our body needs fuel to maintain energy levels. Hunger doesn't correspond with emotional stimuli or impulses; it's simply a basic instinct of our body to function. Appetite, on the other hand, appears suddenly with a sense of urgency and is often triggered by emotions. Most often, it's associated with a craving as you often want a specific type of food: chocolate cake, a slice of pizza, or buttery popcorn. When appetite drives eating versus hunger, it can result in taking in unnecessary calories and a corresponding production of excess fat in the body. All of this rolled together creates feelings of guilt or sadness in consuming the food, gaining weight, or feeling bloated and sick.

Our bodies send us signals to eat, but if we mix up the signal of hunger with that of appetite, things can get out of balance. Often, appetite is triggered by a desire to eat for happiness, boredom, stress, or anxiety. The problem is food is easy to find, all you have to do is open the fridge, or hop in your car and drive to a nearby restaurant. It's hard not to give in to food temptations when your emotional state is overwhelmed, but it's important that we listen to the signals from our body, not our emotional state, when deciding whether or not to eat.

It's been transformative for me to learn to listen to my body and the cues it sends me. Our bodies send us cues when we're tired, in need of certain nutrients, sick, and in pain. Ignoring these signs can lead to illness and disease. After I achieved appetite correction, I realized I didn't need nearly as much food as I was taking in each day. I started to listen to my body when it was full and started to pay attention more to what was triggering me to want to eat. Between intermittent fasting and mindful eating, the weight started to fall off and I started to break my lifelong attachment to food as a constant source of pleasure. Mindful eating encourages a different approach to food that can help to overcome a habit often associated with trauma.

# Chapter 6

# Creative Expression

Creative expression comes in many forms such as theater, music, dance, photography, and painting. I'll focus on the forms of creative expression I used through different stages of my healing journey: drawing, painting, poetry, and dance. Having a creative way to express yourself is important in healing from trauma. If drawing, poetry, and dance aren't your thing, don't worry; there are many other ways to spark creativity.

For those of us who've experienced trauma, we may recognize that some of our thoughts are irrational, but we can't help it. I can't even count how many times people have told me that I'm being irrational. They don't realize that even though you shouldn't feel a certain way, you still do. As, Dr. Bessel van der Kolk says, "You cannot reason yourself out of your trauma. Your cognition can't override your thoughts."[9] This is where creative expression is helpful. One way is to journal about your feelings, which I'll cover in the next chapter. I found that working through my thoughts on paper gives me insight I couldn't access before. Instead of writing, you might prefer to express your emotions through art. Drawing can be helpful if you cannot come up with the words to describe your feelings. You can use the lines, shapes, textures, and the colors and motions of the pencil to express what you feel. Dance can also be great because you can incorporate singing, screaming, or crying as loud or as soft as you want. You can move your body in the ways it's craving to release the internal turmoil boiling up inside of you.

Creative expression is full of positive benefits for both the body and the mind. First, creativity is a natural antidepressant. When you complete a creative task, your brain is filled with dopamine, the hormone that makes you feel great! The burst of dopamine gives you a more positive outlook on the world around you, thus providing you with greater levels of happiness. Second, it can also boost your self-esteem. Who doesn't feel good when they finish a project, step back, and feel pride in their work? You get a sense of personal achievement when you create something out of nothing. Most importantly, creative expression requires that you use parts of your brain that don't often get used in day-to-day tasks. Creative outlets help you find your flow, which is the space where you become so absorbed in the activity that you forget about the negative, stressful, or anxious thoughts that swirl around too often after trauma.

Creative expression can give you the opportunity to develop a skill you can be proud of. You might even consider selling your products at craft fairs or on Etsy. But it's not about making money; it's about finding a purpose. Maybe the craft brings a smile to your face. Maybe it brings a smile to the face of others. Or maybe it brings you into connection with others who also enjoy your same creative outlet.

# Drawing and Painting

I loved to draw as a child and in my teenage years. Around 16 years of age, I learned to paint and grew particularly fond of oil painting. I'm so grateful to my high school art teacher, Ms. JoAnn Soloski, and a local artist in my hometown, Janice Sayward, for embracing my budding talent. They provided an outlet to focus on beauty coming from me rather than hurt and sadness.

My sister, Christina, loves calla lilies. I did a painting for her birthday in January 2009 that I titled, "The Fading Memory". I did this painting after Stan died. Even though I did the painting for her, I couldn't help but tie in my own emotions as I painted. I was reliving traumas I hadn't thought about in years. I was starting to question what was real and what was not.

The painting had three frames of calla lilies. The first frame had three flowers and two leaves. The second frame had two flowers and three leaves. The third frame had one flower and four leaves. The flowers were in different stages of opening from one frame to another. The changes in the number of flowers and what they looked like model our memories and how our memories may have new components or parts that might be deleted over time.

The part of our brain that has an important role in speech production is Broca's area. Unfortunately, this area of the brain can be impacted after trauma. This makes it difficult for you to express your feelings with written or spoken words after trauma and when you recall memories of the trauma, even long after it occurred. That's why creative expression can be so beneficial in processing feelings that you can't get out with words.

# Try It Yourself: Drawing

The following drawing exercise is adapted from *The Transformation: Discovering Wholeness and Healing After Trauma* by James S. Gordon, MD, and used with permission from Dr. Gordon.[10]

We'll do three Drawings. All you need is three sheets of blank paper—8½" by 11" is fine—and crayons or magic markers (which I like better because they're so bright and bold). Do the Drawings quickly. "First thought, best thought," as the Zen Buddhists say. That way the Drawings are likely to be uncensored, authentic, surprising, revealing. Drawings are calling your shy imagination, your intuition, off the bench, to play a creative guiding role in your life.

You'll take about five minutes for each Drawing... [Set a timer if that helps you focus on the art rather than the time. You may feel self-conscious about your drawings, but remember, these drawings are for you and no one else. If, like most, you're unskilled at drawing, it's okay to draw stick figures, abstractions, or something other than a person in your drawings. Begin by closing your eyes and taking a few deep, cleansing breaths. Consider starting with the three-part breath from Chapter 3: Meditation.]

Now open your eyes and do the first Drawing. It's of "Yourself." Don't think about what this means. Just get started. Let your hand take the lead. This first Drawing will get you wrestling with, maybe even laughing at, your self-consciousness. And it will get you out there and down on paper. This is not about skill. No grades. No judgment. Just do it.

Once you're done with Drawing #1, you'll likely say, "Oh yeah, that's me—more or less." Now put this first paper aside.

The second Drawing is "You with your biggest problem." Though this might be quite painful, it's always useful. It's good to identify a problem, even if it's only one among many, to make it real and concrete. Putting it out there on the page, you've removed it from the confused, troubled mass that has filled your mind and maybe overwhelmed you. You can, quite literally, see what you're dealing with.

Again, take a few deep breaths. Now do it...

The third Drawing is "You with your problem solved." "Impossible," you may protest. "I've just lost my job and have no prospects" or "My husband died, and my children don't love me." Don't worry. This is not about listing logical possibilities. It's about letting your imagination come up with possibilities. It's about letting your imagination come up with its answer. Once again, just do it. Allow your intuition to guide you to the colors, to move your hand...

After you've finished your own Drawings, take some time to look at them.

What do you see on the page? Notice the forms, the

colors, the relative size and position of the figures. What's the mood of each Drawing?

Are you surprised at the first picture, the way you drew yourself? So small or big? Without feet or missing a head? Smiling or sad? Alone or with others? What does this Drawing have to tell you about the way you see yourself? What's missing in your picture of yourself? Have you neglected to include aspects of your character, perhaps admirable qualities?

What about the problem that emerged in the second Drawing? Is it an exquisitely painful portrait of life-dominating loss? A predictable acknowledgement of limitations and constraint, like a clock, prison bars, or stacks of unread assignments? An astonishing gift from the unconscious...? Were you aware of it before? Does seeing it on the page help you understand and deal with it?

And what do you think about the third Drawing, the solution? Is there intelligence, even wisdom, in it? Does it point you in a new direction?

It may be a practical solution: reaching out to a friend to overcome loneliness, going to the gym to relieve stress and feel better about your body, sharing shame and feeling it loosen its grip. It may involve...confronting what you've been avoiding. Your solution may take you deep inside...to regroup emotionally. It may point you to a new commitment to life and caring... Take some time to consider the solution you drew.

Are there action steps you may want to take?...

Countless stressed-out people of all ages have followed the guidance of their Drawings to open spaces, energizing physical and creative activity, the welcome company of forgotten friends and family, to a new commitment to helping themselves and others. They have been able to embrace what they've drawn—both the pain and constraint of their problem and the expansive satisfying third picture of what their lives might be.

Sometimes, they do it right away. Sometimes, it's a gradual process.

You may want to put your Drawings on your wall or refrigerator, or next to your computer, where they can welcome you with possibility and encourage your progress. In any case, hold on to them. Put them somewhere safe...

You can do this set of Drawings often—whenever you're dealing with difficulty, overwhelmed by fear, uncertain of how to act, unable to do what needs to be done, or simply in need of an image of Hope.

I first did these pictures myself at Dr. Gordon's workshop, "Healing Life's Inevitable Traumas" I attended in 2019. The exercise was very profound for me.

My first drawing:

This is the face I portray to the world – happy and bubbly with bright eyes and a big smile. Not long after I went to this workshop, I listened to the book, *Essence of the Upanishads*, by Eknath Easwaran.[11] Hearing how we focus so much on the external appearance of ourselves and others hit close to home and made me think back to this first drawing. The same day I was listening to this book and thinking about this drawing, I saw a young woman at work dressed in a flashy, shimmering, gold-colored blouse with matching shoes. I was mesmerized by the shine. But I couldn't help but think, *What is she trying to prevent people from seeing on the inside?* I've always enjoyed wearing flashy clothes. As I reflected on the book and my own life, I realized that by trying to captivate people with my shiny appearance and bubbly personality, they'll be too distracted to see my insecurities, imperfections, negative thoughts, and how much I'm hurting inside. It's the same reason I've always approached the world with a cheerful smile, even when I felt like I was dying inside.

One day, while chatting with a colleague, I confessed that I struggled with anxiety and depression. He looked at me stunned. He said, "Really?! You?! I never would have guessed that. You always look so happy and chipper and you've accomplished so much." Like most people who only know the person I am today, he had no idea of the multiple traumas I experienced in my life and the number of times I contemplated suicide. People who are just getting to know me don't see my past. They don't know about the sleepless nights I still have from time to time as I play reruns in my mind of my most difficult life experiences.

Most of us hide pain with smiles. We say we're doing well because we know, deep down, most people don't want to hear the truth. People are often shocked by what I'm willing to share about my past. But it's important to know, especially in the days of social media, where people only show the highlight reels of their life, that we all have a hidden story. We must start giving people permission to speak their truth.

My second drawing:

Even though I have always showed a smile to the world, for many days of my life, I felt as though I were dying inside. I have fewer days like this as time goes on, but I still show a smile to the world when I'm in physical pain, or I'm overwhelmed by all the work I have to do. People just don't want to hear about it. When people ask you how you're doing, they don't really want to know. "How are you?" has become a casual greeting that you say even when you're walking by a person, with no intention of stopping to hear the answer.

When I did this drawing, I was going through a difficult time at home with my boyfriend at the time. I was also dealing with health concerns. I had a habit of coming into my job each morning and cheerfully saying, "Good morning!" One day, when things were particularly bad, I didn't say anything when I came into the office. I just went right to my desk and tried my best to focus on my work. A little while later, one of my colleagues walked by and said, "Oh, I didn't know you were here. I didn't hear you say, 'Good morning.' I look forward to that each morning." I know she meant no harm by it. But what she didn't realize is that she was encouraging me to repeat a harmful pattern of putting on a smile when I felt like my soul was shattering into a million pieces. She didn't realize that at the age of 13 I was told by someone I was supposed to trust that if I couldn't grow up and learn how to control my emotions after I finally talked about the sexual abuse I had been suffering for months that I wasn't welcome back to their home. She didn't realize that I had learned from an early age to stuff my sadness into the darkest recesses of my being so I could shine like a bright light to the world just to make everyone else happy and to prevent their discomfort. So, to continue the trend of swallowing my own discomfort to prevent the discomfort of others, from that point on, even if I felt depressed, right before I would walk into my office door, I would stand up straight, put a smile on my face, and cheerfully say, "Good morning!"

My third drawing:

This is how I want to feel and approach the world. Happy and at peace, but not over-the-top. I want to smile most days, but I don't want it to be forced. I want it to be a genuine expression of how I feel inside.

Since I did these drawings, I've started to become aware of the face I present to the world. I realize that I'm alright with showing the bright-eyed, cheerful smile to the world, because I'm bubbly by nature and generally excited by life. But I'm now cognizant to show this bright smile because it's a true reflection of how I'm feeling on the inside at that moment and not me projecting the Stephanie that I think the world wants to see.

I drew exactly the pictures I needed to draw that day. I was somewhat frustrated by not having enough time to finish my drawings. However, the reason behind the time limit is to prevent you from overthinking it. It forces you to draw exactly what's on your mind.

These drawings reinforced for me the importance of working through my emotions instead of continuing to push them down. As I said to the group, "I feel sad all of the time." My inner critic started going off, saying things like, *Really, Stephanie, you aren't sad all the time*, with a little taste of disgust at my embellishment.

But as I later reflected about the whole experience, I realized the reason I don't feel sad literally all the time is because of how I'm never still. I'm always doing something. My poor cats, especially, Molly, will try to follow me around the house for a while. They stop once they realize I'm not going to be still. Finally, once I'm still and they feel I'm settled, they'll come and sit by me or lay with me. I'm like a jack rabbit, bouncing all over the place because in my stillness, I realize my deep-rooted sadness. Then, my demons come out to play. It's why I work so much, overeat, and fill my open space with audiobooks. That's why meditation has been so important for me because it forces me to be still.

Through these drawings, I finally understand why I needed to move through the pain and not keep pushing it down and storing it. I've mistakenly thought all these years that by ignoring my past, it wouldn't affect me. But the truth is that it was always there, like termites eating away at the internal structure of my body and mind.

By working through the trauma and not suppressing it, you can move to the point where you can say, "It's over." The goal is to be able to tell your story as something that happened way back in the past and not like it's happening right now. I appreciated hearing Dr. van der Kolk say, "You need to revisit the past, but it needs to be approached from a place of compassion and knowing that was then and this is now."[9]

Your traumatic experiences are just a small part of the overall experiences you may have in your life. But it's so easy for your trauma to become your whole life story. Your identity. It can make you miss the beautiful opportunities available along the journey because you didn't believe that a new chapter in your life could be written.

## Poetry

Poetry is what I turned to during early adolescence, which happened to be the years in which my traumas were most numerous and catapulted me into a life of many more traumas to follow. It was a devastating time for me. Poetry saved me during these years. It allowed me to express emotions I didn't even fully understand yet.

I wrote about my feelings about my parents getting divorced and both of them eventually remarrying. I wrote about two of my classmates in school, from a graduating class of 16, dying. One was a boy I had slept with and the first of the three men I've been with who've died. I wrote about being raped. I wrote about someone coming up behind me and putting a knife to my throat. I wrote about love. I wrote about sadness, rage, and fear. I wrote whatever I felt and needed to get out. I have pages upon pages of poems. I spewed my soul into words on paper that I was never able to say out loud. This process saved me during some of the most difficult years of my life.

I haven't written any poems for many years and as I read through the poems I wrote as a teenager, all I can think is that if people would read them, they wouldn't think they were very good. But it was never about being a good poet. It was about expressing what was in my heart and head that I couldn't get out in any other way. I didn't feel I had anyone to turn to, so this provided me a release.

What I found most interesting about the poems is how most of them were focused on love, how I wanted to love and be loved. I'll never forget when a past boyfriend told me that all I really wanted is to be loved. I didn't know it was so obvious I was seeking love because it wasn't obvious to me. As I read back through my old poems, I realize the desire to love and be loved has driven many of my actions since childhood. To be pretty enough, smart enough, accomplished enough, to just be enough so I would be lovable.

Some poems made me sad to read because I remembered that I have felt broken for most of my life. I called this poem, "My Life." It was dated May 9, 1997. I was 15 years old.

My life is like a dirt road.

It has potholes,

Which I keep fallin' in.

It has rocks,

Like the ones I keep trippin' over.

Every turn I take,

There's a dead end.

Just like my life.

Most of my poems never touched directly on my traumas. It makes sense because I never really even acknowledged my traumas until my early 20s. I went through my life pretending all those things didn't happen to me. But I did have a series of dark poems I wrote around the age of 15. I had to think about the time frame and what had happened during the year 1997. Still in the year 2021, as I'm finishing this book, it creates a sinking feeling in my chest when I think about that year. That year sealed my silence and catapulted me into a downward spiral. The final time I was going to ever tell anyone what happened to me. Before the age of 15, I had already been sexually violated numerous times by five separate men.

One night, not long after I turned 15, I was at my friend CJ's house at his birthday party and that number climbed to seven. CJ's mother, her boyfriend, and one of their friends were playing cards and feeding us Aftershock cinnamon liqueur. To this day, I cannot stomach the smell from it. I probably did 20 shots of it from the time I arrived in the late afternoon until I passed out sometime late in the night. I remember making out with two of the teenage boys who were there that I had crushes on. But I also remember the older male who didn't live there, trapped me in the bathroom and was taking my clothes off while he fingered me. Just then, the mother's boyfriend flings open the door, starts screaming at his friend, and chases him out of the house. I remember later falling down the stairs because I was so drunk and not waking up until I realized that someone's fingers were inside of me. It was the mother's boyfriend. My supposed savior was just saving me for himself. I don't remember much after that other than him kissing me. The next morning, I could see that CJ's mother was completely disgusted by me. I could only remember flashes of what happened to me that night, but her look just told me that I should feel ashamed of myself. So, I said that I was sorry. She said, "You knew exactly what you were doing and got everything you asked for." I found it astonishing. I never actually added up the numbers until

2019 when I first started going through my poems. By the age of 15, I was sexually violated by seven different men, all adult men except for one who was a teenager. I was also sexually violated again when I was 19, increasing the total to 8 different males who had sexually violated me during my life.

I use the phrase "sexual violence" to encompass the variety of abuses I suffered. Six guys violated me with some form of penetration. One was molestation at the age of 9 or 10 by someone very close to me and another man very close to me who exposed himself to me when I was in my early teens. Even without penetration these two men caused me the most pain because of who they were and the constant fear of the abuses escalating during most of my young life. The numbers don't include the countless times I had been sexually harassed and touched inappropriately, copping a feel of my breasts, grabbing my ass, or trying to kiss me as I pushed them away. But I don't count those because there were so many more things that were worse than that, it seems insignificant, even though I know it's not. It's sad to think I became so numb to unwanted words and touch that these other numbers don't even register in my mind.

It's hard to believe I wrote poems in which I called myself a whore when I was 14 years old. Yet, I also couldn't believe that at 14, I wrote poems with titles like, "I'm a Kinky Girl," "Give It to Me Good," and "All Night" that were centered around sex. Reading through these poems brought back a flood of memories I had buried away, memories of going on chatrooms in my early teens with grown men having sexual conversations with me. It's disturbing to think that by 14, I had come to think I was only good as a sex object. Grown men had their way with me. They were teaching me how I was expected to serve men. It's not surprising I became hypersexual and have had sex with more men than I dare to count. I used to pride myself on the fact men regularly told me having sex with me was like having sex with a porn star, that I was unforgettable. Although my lust to be desired sexually has been greatly diminished, I still desire to be remembered by all who meet me. I still have an almost overpowering desire to be seen, to always be the most interesting person in the room, to still be, unforgettable.

## Try It Yourself: Poetry

Write a poem! Begin by letting go of any expectation that your poem should be good. You're not writing this for anyone other than yourself. And it's not important for your poem to rhyme.

You can start out by simply writing about what you're feeling. If you're in pain, write about your pain. If you're feeling filled with hope, write about that. But, if you write about your pain, I encourage you to also write about a way out of your pain. Maybe start with writing down your hurt and pain in one poem. Then for the second poem write about what you're grateful for in your life. Then in the third poem, create a poem that gives you hope for the future.

## Dance

I used to regularly put music on and dance around my house. This was very important in my healing after Stan died. In fact, movement, specifically shaking, is a natural way for the body to release tension and return to normal homeostasis. After a life-threatening event, animals naturally shake to release the built-up tension. In this way, they literally release the trauma from their bodies. Humans, on the other hand, don't always know how to dissipate stress after a traumatic experience. We release huge amounts of stress hormones through the fight-or-flight response which help us to escape danger (or deal with traumatic experiences). But throughout our socialization, humans have forgotten how to recalibrate their nervous systems by shaking it off and getting back to normal. Therefore, our emotions become frozen inside of us, especially with situations involving abuse. Long-term suppression of feelings manifests itself in chronic mental, emotional, and physical distress. Dance is a beautiful way to release tension from our body. Dance allows us to release the stress versus burying it down deep where it can fester and lead to illness.

The poetry section of this book was difficult for me to write. It brought up the most emotions for me. That same night I wrote that section, I told my boyfriend at the time, the revelation I had while writing about the number of men I've been sexually violated by. I cried a little, he hugged me. Then I listened to music that made me happy and wanted to sing. Then I transitioned to music that made me want to sing and dance. I felt like I was shaking off all the yuck that came up while combing through my old poems.

## Try It Yourself: Dance

Put on your favorite music in a location where you'll have privacy. You want the freedom to move and sing, without feeling constrained by the concerns of judgment from onlookers. As you engage in regular dance, you might be more willing to dance in front of others, but in the beginning, it's best to be by yourself so you can really focus on listening to your body. I also encourage you to dance in a room without a mirror or dance facing away from the mirror. We can be our harshest critics. You don't want to restrict yourself during dance because you start criticizing your dancing skills and the way you look.

This isn't about being good. This is about allowing your body to move the way it wants. We're always restricting ourselves in fear of judgment, but this causes us to bury feelings deep inside of us. Dancing allows you the opportunity to let it out. As the music plays, listen to your body and how it's telling you to move. Think of where you're holding back and see where you can let it go. If you want to be sensual, be sensual. Society tells us that being sensual is wrong, but it's an inherent part of our being.

Are you feeling called to sing or hum along to the music? If so, go for it! Again, it's not about being a good singer, it's about listening to the signals your body is trying to send you. You don't have to understand it; you just have to listen. I encourage you to create music playlists on YouTube, Amazon Music, Spotify, or a similar type of application. You can even categorize your playlists based on the type of feeling you want to get from the songs, such as empowerment, strength, or happiness.

I understand how uncomfortable it might be. You might be thinking, what if someone is able to see me? I'll never forget when I attended Unleash the Power Within (UPW) with Tony Robbins in Los Angeles. Being surrounded by 15,000 people all looking to change their lives was amazing. Now, I'll openly admit that many things about the event were odd and uncomfortable. It was a life-changing experience for me, so I was able to overlook the intense marketing efforts, which made me uncomfortable and sometimes annoyed.

But other things that made me uncomfortable were really coming from inside of me. I left my hotel room around 6:30 am on the first day and didn't get back to my hotel until after 2:00 am and turned around and did it again the next day. To keep our energy high during the intense 4-day experience, the speakers regularly had us getting up and dancing, screaming, and hugging strangers. I was surrounded by people going crazy and getting really excited. I was surprised I was able to handle the extreme stimulation. Lights flashing, music on blast, cheering. It was like being at a rock concert. I asked one of the volunteers at the event for a pair of ear plugs and they were nice enough to get some for me. The ear plugs helped me survive the event.

I have it ingrained in my mind that what we were doing was odd and unacceptable. I found myself being rigid when we were first being told to "Shake that ass!" But by the end of the event, I was shaking my ass every time we were signaled to do so. By the end, I was smiling, loosened up, and more comfortable in my own skin. What helped me loosen up was sharing some very personal thoughts and feelings that came up during various activities with at least one person sitting next to me. After my first partner became very vulnerable with what she was sharing with me, it just made something click inside of me. I felt like I could let go. After that, I started to become more comfortable with being me. The next time the music came on, I started to dance like crazy.

We tend to be far too rigid because of restrictions placed upon us by parents, teachers, and society. When that's compounded by traumas that cause us to tense and brace ourselves, it's hard to relax. I've come to appreciate events like UPW that really encourage you to let loose and move outside of your comfort zone. Recently, while shopping in Walmart, a Christmas song came on that just made me very happy. I started to sing to myself and had this sudden urge to start dancing around. I stopped myself because I knew that wouldn't be considered socially acceptable, but I did sing a little and walked around smiling because I was happy. As I was picking out some bananas, a man came up to me, looked me directly in the eyes, smiled, and said, "I'm sure you'd like to dance right now." I smiled and said, "I'd love to dance all around the aisles right now." He looked at me half like it made him happy to hear and half like he was wondering if I was a raving lunatic. It's viewed as socially acceptable to walk around with your shoulders slumped, not making eye contact, or in your own world with earbuds in, but it's seen as strange to walk around smiling and happy. I get that a lot when I'm traveling, especially when I was traveling around Russia for a month. Most people don't walk around smiling there, so they weren't sure what to think of me. In Tanzania, on the other hand, people welcomed my smiling, but commented on how most Americans aren't usually that way.

## Activity

Next time you're out, smile! Look around you and notice the posture and facial expressions of people. Are they happy? Are they smiling? Are they moving or dancing or have a bounce in their step? Or do you notice them looking down, hunched over, hurrying through life without looking around? Think about how you can enjoy the world around you more by expressing your own emotions rather than keeping them bottled up. Just like animals shake off tension, we humans can do the same. And we can also use movement to express our joy and happiness too!

# Chapter 7

# Journaling

As I read through my journals while writing this book, I couldn't help but notice how much my handwriting has changed over the years and how my handwriting changes based on the mood I'm in. It was also interesting to see trends in the thoughts, feelings, and habits that haven't changed much over the years. I continue to struggle with my sugar addiction. I still struggle with the feeling that I'm insignificant.

Some people find immense value in journaling every day. I personally journal when I feel called to do so. Sometimes, my mind is filled with thoughts that I just need to get out. As I was reviewing my journals, I found I would journal for a few days in a row and then not write again for a few months. I wish I had written in my journals more often. When living in the moment of an experience, we think that moment will be unforgettable. But with so many new experiences and emotions filling our mind and body with inputs every day, it stands to reason that we can't remember it all indefinitely.

I've used journaling to work through my thoughts for over 25 years. I have journaled for many reasons during this time. Sometimes, it's to express feelings of frustration or despair. Other times, it's to make note of goals or changes I'm wanting to make in my life. Sometimes, I journal to acknowledge how far I've come.

Having the ability to read back through my thoughts over the decades of my life has reinforced how far I've come. I can't believe some of the things I wrote. It broke my heart to recount all the times I was in complete despair. At my worst, I included just basic cleaning of myself and my home as something to be proud of.

Journal entry on May 30, 2011, 12:11am

*I was prompted to write in this journal because I just found this show "Addicted" on TV that made me start thinking about why I overeat and why I sleep with so many men. What's the void that I'm trying to fill...?...? I don't really know.*

Journal entry on February 17, 2012

*Today I tested negative for HIV. What a relief. Today was one of the most nerve-racking days of my life waiting for those test results to come back. Why do I do these things to myself? I'm so proud of myself for getting tested because it was so scary, but upset with myself at the same time for making so many bad choices that put me at risk for even possibly contracting it in the first place.*

Entries like this one make me reflect on the numerous times I've had heart palpitations waiting to receive the results from HIV and pregnancy tests. It makes me think of all the times as a teenager I used to pound on my stomach when I thought I might be pregnant. It makes me think about all the close calls I've had. How many times I thanked God when the pregnancy tests came back negative. But what an interesting turn of events it was when at 35, I wanted to have a child and couldn't. I would look at the pregnancy test wanting it to now be positive and it never happened.

Journal entry on May 13, 2018

*I think I push myself so hard to be successful to make sense of all the bad that has happened to me. I don't want to acknowledge that these events were random. I'm not special. I wasn't "chosen" to experience these hardships so I could better lead others through theirs. I feel that I've always been judged harshly by others, so I'm always aiming to accomplish so much to prove everyone wrong. But what if the only real judgment I have ever faced has come from within? What if I'm just pushing myself so hard to prove to myself that I'm worthy, that I'm good enough, that I'm lovable? The judgment I pass onto others is likely a reflection of the way I judge myself.*

I have hoarding tendencies, which means I have a difficult time letting go of items, as I might have a use for them in the future or they possess a sentimental value. Over the past few years, I've been working on this and have been slowing going through my belongings and discarding and donating those items that no longer serve me. This was my journal entry on June 24, 2020:

*I used to acquire so many things, trying to fill a void inside of me. In addition to moving multiple times, I used to redecorate every time I moved. I kept thinking that changing my external environment would change my internal environment. It did, but it never lasted long. So, I would run away again to the next job, the new home, or to another exotic location, only to find that I could never run far enough away from my past. I could never escape it. It was a part of me. It has taken me years to learn that my traumas didn't make me weak, but they made me strong. It has taken me years to embrace a past that I cannot change to use as fuel to move toward a future of my design.*

Sometimes I write in my journal when I've reached a turning point in my life. This is what I wrote in my journal entry on May 10, 2020, which I consider to be a turning point:

*I was working on a worksheet on beliefs for one of my online coaching programs and I provided an example of the belief, "I'm unlovable." This was an easy example for me, as I have regularly felt this way myself. This is why I've always wanted a man to continuously remind me that he loves me. After 7 years with [my boyfriend at the time] I've gotten better at not needing constant reminders from him. What was interesting was right as I was writing this belief, [my boyfriend] came upstairs to have me listen to a song and we slow-danced together. It really was a special moment. Afterwards, instead of going right back to my work, I decided to complete my daily gratitude practice. I focused on how grateful I am for [him]. Then I thought about countless different ways I've tried to sabotage our relationship, trying to prove the belief about myself true, that I'm unlovable. I've hurt him in so many different ways that I'm ashamed of, and he has stayed through it all. It was like a lightbulb went off for me. I had never put it together until that very moment how much he truly does love me. I had been fighting to prove myself right that I was unlovable and he was fighting to prove that I was lovable and I never saw it until that very moment.*

This was a big deal for me. I've engaged in so many self-destructive sexual relationships to stop feeling that I am unlovable and to find proof that I am lovable. I have put strain on my current and past relationships by requiring them to make up for the love I didn't feel toward myself.

On August 20, 2019, I used my journal to reflect on the session I had with my therapist the day before. I was telling my therapist how I felt like I was depressed. He told me that he felt that I was feeling sorrow and not depression. Over the next 24 hours I spent a lot of time reflecting on the differences between sorrow and depression and where the sense of sorrow could be coming from if that's what it was. I used my journal to identify all the things I had recently lost.

- I was mourning the loss of a job that I had for nine years and chose to leave three months prior.
- I was mourning the loss of a relationship with my intimate partner at the time when our relationship was ending.
- I was mourning the loss of my hair. I had very long hair for my entire life and chopped it all off five months prior.
- I was mourning the loss of climbing the tallest mountains in the world. After my unsuccessful attempt of Ojos in the beginning of the year, I had made the decision to no longer pursue the seven summits.

Journaling about all that I was mourning allowed me the opportunity to reflect on the new stage of my life that I was entering. I told myself, "It's okay if I take time to not focus on serving others. It's okay to focus on me, who I am, and who I want to be in the next stage of my life."

Journal entry on May 13, 2012
- *I need to accept that I may never look like a super model.*

- *I need to accept that no matter how skinny I get, I might always still have some cellulite.*
- *I need to stop being so overly critical of myself.*
- *I need to remind myself that there's more to me than just my looks. I'm not defined by my looks.*
- *I need to feel more comfortable when going to the pool.*
- *I need to feel more comfortable when seeing someone who hasn't seen me since I've put on all this weight. (I weighed over 220 pounds during this period of my life.)*

As I reflect on this and the title of this book, *Transformation After Trauma*, that's truly what I've experienced, a *transformation*. I feel like I'm a different person. Although I still have some of the same struggles with body image, overeating, and overfunctioning, my life today is barely recognizable. I'm no longer the self-destructing, self-loathing, suicidal Stephanie. Through journaling, I can create the new story of Stephanie. I get to reflect on who I want her to be and create a plan on how to make that happen.

Journal entry on May 18, 2010:
  *Things I'm going to ask for God's assistance with:*
- *The ability to love myself.*
- *The ability to not self-destruct.*
- *The ability to not use men as a form of self-destruction.*
- *Finding a good man, one who I'll not only be attracted to, but will be worthy of my trust and loyalty.*
  - *Finding the man I'll marry.*
- *The ability to focus on my goals in life.*

- *The energy to exercise so I can stay healthy and so my external beauty can match my internal beauty.*
- *The ability to ask for help even when I don't think I need it because I can't do it all on my own.*

What will your new story be? Who will you be when you're no longer saddled by your past, when you're no longer defined by your trauma? Who will you be if you're no longer a survivor? Who will you be when you release the terms that define you based on your trauma?

I've never liked using the term "survivor" for myself. The more I heal, and the stronger I get, the more I resist using such terms to describe myself. I know some people feel the word "survivor" is empowering. But I view the word as a way for someone to still identify themselves as a victim. If you continue to identify yourself as a victim, you'll continue to be trapped by your past.

The traumas of being sexual violated by 8 men, attacked from behind at knife point, and finding my significant other dead are all part of me. But they no longer anchor me and the way I define myself. They no longer limit me. I refuse to give any of those men or circumstances one more ounce of power and one more ounce of my life energy. They've stolen so much from me. I'm not going to give them more power by saying I'll always be your victim. I've, instead, broken my chains from those memories and have risen like a phoenix. If I can rise from the ashes, so can you. If I can create a new version of myself moving forward, so can you. Pick up your pen and paper and get to creating the new you!

## Try It Yourself: Journaling

Stream of consciousness is a form of writing where you simply put your pen to paper and write anything that comes to your mind. Don't censor anything. If you're concerned with someone else reading your journal, remember there are locking journals available on Amazon. I particularly like the journals with a combination lock, so I don't have to worry about keeping track of the key. There are also journaling apps like Penzu that require a password to open. You can also just write freely and then throw it away or shred it. You don't always have to keep your journals, but it can be helpful if you want a written record of your healing journey.

If you struggle with what to write, some ideas are to write about what you're grateful for, what you're proud of, short-term and long-term goals, and how your past is showing up in your present life.

Dr. Peter Levine talks about how in modern cultures, people are taught to be heroic by continuing on and pushing through regardless of the severity of our symptoms. We rationalize events and downplay their impact on us by coming across as if the event were almost insignificant. In fact, we're socialized to pretend as if nothing really happened to us at all. But according to him, this is a terrible injustice we do to ourselves. By not recognizing the trauma, we merely entrench it in ourselves, freezing our nervous system, and setting ourselves up for a disaster.[12] We need to find the appropriate tools to help us acknowledge our experiences, especially those that are traumatic. In this way, journaling can help you express rather than suppress or deny your feelings in a safe space where you can choose to share or not share with others.

# Chapter 8

# Loving Your Body

Self-care is such an important part of healing from trauma. Self-care, in the form of showing your body love, is of critical importance to those of us who've been sexually or physically abused. It's also essential for those who have physical reminders of their trauma from war, accident, injury by a victimizer, or a medical procedure. When you begin to feel your body is disgusting and repulsive, and you're afraid of anyone getting close to your body, it's essential to show your body love. The ways that have worked best for me are baths and massage.

In 2016, when I was in Turkey, I had a traditional Turkish bath and massage from a very kind and gentle woman. The whole process started with the bath. It was the first time I had ever had another person bathe me. I was naked except for this slinky, see-though thong they gave me to wear during the bath. I couldn't help but focus on the rolls in my stomach and how disgusted this woman must be by me. I was so self-conscious about my body during both the bath and the massage. But she was so sweet to me. She knew I was uncomfortable so in a soft, gentle voice, she would continually say, "It's okay. It's okay." To this day, I'm so grateful for her reassurances. The bath finished with her using a foaming bag. It was the most exhilarating feeling. It was this whoosh of suds across my body. I had never experienced anything like it before or since. I often reminisce about that sensation. It was like magic. I'm so grateful that I let myself be vulnerable enough to allow such a beautiful experience into my life. After the bath came the massage and I felt truly blessed by the whole experience.

Since then, I try to get at least one massage each time I'm traveling to a new country to experience the different styles of massage. I received a massage in Chile after my summit attempt of Ojos del Salado and tears came down my face. I was filled with emotion because I was grateful to have somebody who used their hands to touch me in a way that didn't hurt me.

Massage can be very helpful, especially for people who have been victimized by the hands of others. It can help you build a sense of trust in other people and know people can touch you without harming you. It took me a long time to understand it's okay to be touched, that I deserve to be touched, and people can touch my body in a way that won't hurt me. Massage can let you know you're not too disgusting to be touched, which is something I've often battled with. In fact, that knowledge has been game changing for me.

There are a whole host of massage benefits for both the body and the mind beyond our healing from trauma. Cortisol is a hormone that is released into the body in response to stress. It elevates your heart rate and blood pressure, which can have detrimental long-term effects on the body. Massage decreases cortisol while it increases the release of dopamine, serotonin, and oxytocin, all the feel-good chemicals.

Physical pain is a byproduct of trauma for many people, including myself. I continue to struggle with physical pain, and massage can help decrease that pain. Many people who've experienced trauma experience physical pain, as their bodies are always preparing for action. When the body is always preparing to fight or run away, our muscles remain tense and create palpable knots, which a massage therapist can often release.

When getting a massage, it's important to tell the practitioner if something doesn't feel right. When you go in for a massage, they may ask, "Do you like deep or light pressure?" and you may not know. If they start experimenting with deeper pressure and it hurts, it's completely okay to ask them to lighten the pressure. Let them know up front about any concerns you may have so they know where you're coming from. Don't take off more clothes than you're comfortable with. It's also perfectly acceptable to request a massage therapist of a specific gender. When you're ready to try a professional massage, I encourage you to start with a male or female therapist, based on your level of comfort. For years, I only had female massage therapists, but now I'm comfortable with a male therapist.

Meet yourself where you currently are. Try not to be hard on yourself for not being farther along on your journey. Depending on the type of trauma you've experienced, being touched by another person may present difficulty for you, but you can overcome it!

## *Try It Yourself: Loving Your Body*

I encourage you to start with taking warm baths first if you're overwhelmed by the thought of someone else touching you during a massage. Buy a new loofa and some great smelling bath gel. Or pick out a relaxing bath oil or bomb to splurge on yourself a bit.

Once you start to show yourself love and discover you're deserving, you'll be more likely to open yourself up to new opportunities to show yourself love. You can progress up to getting a professional massage by starting with someone you trust giving you a massage. You don't have to lie down on a table and remove your clothing. Maybe just start with them putting lotion on your hands or feet. Then, if you're comfortable, you can have them progress up your arms and legs and have them stop if you become too uncomfortable. Over time, you'll begin to see that you can be touched, and no harm will come to you.

# Chapter 9

# Connections to Community

I gave my team quite a scare on Day 5 of my Kili climb in 2017. On these long treks, it's common to frog hop with other groups. You pass them and while you rest, they pass you. This can continue many times over if the groups have a similar pace. During the climb on this day, I saw the same porter many times. I took notice of him because while waiting in the long line of people going up the Barranco Wall, he was literally roaring. He had already said "Hi" to me during the times I had seen him earlier in the day, so I smiled at him when he was roaring. He said, "I am a lion." I saw him a little while later and said, "Oh, you're the lion." I saw him again later and said, "There's the lion." That time, I also asked him his real name, and he replied, "Emmanuel." He was the third Emmanuel I had met so far on this trip, so it was an easy name to remember.

When I was waiting for Prosper, my guide, to register us with the ranger, I saw Emmanuel yet again. Prosper showed him where our tents were in case he wanted to come visit us later. I doubted I would see Emmanuel again, but while I was eating dinner, he came and found me in the dining vestibule in my tent. I was happy to see him because he seemed so nice, his English was good, and it gave me someone to talk to. He broke the boredom of me sitting in my tent by myself.

After a few minutes of talking with Emmanuel, Faustine, my chef, came rushing out of his tent and I could tell he wasn't happy. He said some things to Emmanuel in Swahili. Emmanuel told me he made a mistake and would see me tomorrow on the trail then left.

I still needed to finish my dinner so Faustine came in the tent and sat with me. This wasn't that unusual, as Faustine and I would regularly visit when I was eating. But this time, he sat on the ground peering out of the unzipped opening of my tent at Emmanuel and his friend. Based on his behavior, I could tell that Faustine was concerned about my safety.

After I finished eating, Prosper came to check on me. It was time for my evening medical checkup, but first we started talking about what previously transpired. Prosper explained that to talk with a client from a different company, Emmanuel must get permission first. The reason for the permission is because if something or someone goes missing, they'll know who to look for. I politely explained, "That's a general problem I have. I don't see danger when I should. I generally think people are good and don't want to believe they want to cause me harm. But I should know by now, that's not always the case."

After Prosper left my tent, I reflected on a conversation I had with my boyfriend about a time when he watched me play with my nieces and nephew at a family gathering. He remarked that as he watched me playing with them, he couldn't help but think about the bad things that have happened to me in my life when

I'm so good. He said it's probably because I'm so good that people take advantage of me.

You would think that given the trauma I've experienced in my past, I would be more wary of people who might be out to hurt me. But even as I was conversing with "The Lion," it didn't click. He told me how he wanted to be a guide but didn't have the money to pay for the classes to get certified. Honestly, it never even dawned on me that he might pose a potential threat. I had a fleeting thought he was hoping I would feel bad for him and would want to help him financially. But that thought quickly passed and I went on talking about how maybe the guide company he works for might help him reach his goal. I love learning about the dreams and goals of others and helping them to devise plans to meet those goals. I can get so hyperfocused on certain parts of a conversation that I miss red flags. So, if I'm excited about a part of a conversation, I tend to overlook portions of the conversation that seemed a bit odd. That is, until I have time to reflect on the conversation later.

At first, I don't put up a guard when I meet someone. But after I've had time to evaluate the interaction and ruminate over it, I start to question the interaction and the intentions of the individual. This part has always been the most difficult for me. I love getting to know people, but it's rare that I don't end up questioning what their intentions might be after I've had time to process the interaction.

Experiencing multiple traumas, including abuse by those I trusted and loss of a loved one, has made me put up a huge barrier that prevents people from getting in. I find it interesting though how conflicted I get about this. I have a great desire to get to know people, to make strong connections, but the moment it happens, fear starts to kick in and up goes my guard. I make the barrier around me extra thick to prevent penetration. I've had this desire to get to know people for as long as I can remember, but what led to some of my traumas is men mistaking my curiosity for attraction. I would end up getting hurt because I got too close. Either my boundaries have been too strong, or they've been too lax. It seems that I've always favored one extreme or the other. But the key is to find balance.

Trauma can leave you feeling isolated. This isolation can make it difficult to become in tune with other people. Because of this, I used to gravitate toward those who were in obvious pain. I know how to connect with them. I know they understand pain even without speaking a word about our pain. It's why I gravitated toward men like Stan.

People who haven't experienced trauma usually don't want to hear about trauma. Most of the time, they would prefer to go on believing the world is safe and that terrible things don't happen to people, even though they do. This leads to a deepening sense of isolation for those who've been traumatized. I'll never forget the time when I paid to boost a Facebook post that included a link to a personal story blog post on my website. Facebook actually sent me a message saying this post might not perform as well because some of the content in the post might be difficult for some people to read. Facebook restricted my story from reaching my audience simply because my story was upsetting. I couldn't help but laugh. Imagine the hell that was going on inside of me when I actually experienced multiple traumas! I only included brief snippets of my story and softened it to minimize the chance of triggering readers. Imagine if I actually included everything? It's amazing that even Facebook knows its readers want to pretend these types of horrors don't exist, further creating a sense of isolation for those who experience the trauma.

People who haven't experienced trauma may have a difficult time empathizing with you and your actions or inactions. I have felt so many times in my life as though I lived on a different planet and didn't belong here. I often contemplated that maybe my traumas were punishment for being a foreigner, an invader. It's likely why I'm empathetic to immigrants who are treated as though they don't belong. I've felt like I wasn't and couldn't be accepted as a part of the larger community.

I feel that correctional facilities tend to collect mostly people who are considered to be broken by society. You put people who have chronic trauma in a single place, and they can't help but victimize one another. With little support to work through their traumas, the real reason most people end up in prison in the first place, they'll continue to become victims and victimizers. Many won't become productive members of society because they won't have a sense of community when they come out. The high recidivism rate may be due to feelings of isolation. They don't feel like they belong. So, they go back to the only place that feels like home to them, a place of connection.

## Activity

Make a list of people you can contact if you need to laugh, cry, or just have someone there to listen. If you're prone to retreating inwards when you're particularly depressed and are less likely to reach out when you need it most, find a family member or friend who will reach out regularly just to check in. It's important that you have people who can serve as a lifeline on really hard days.

People like to be connected with me, but I break away the moment I feel they're wanting to get too close, when I feel they're wanting more than I can give. So often, I've gotten caught up in my own pain that I don't feel I have the resources available to give to anyone else.

What's interesting though, is how easily I can connect with people. My sister, Christina, once said that I was a chameleon, as I could talk to anyone, and it's true. I feel comfortable around everyone. I like to believe people are genuinely good, interesting, and have something valuable to share.

Early in our relationship, a long-term boyfriend of mine noticed I was a social butterfly and loved talking with every new person I met. He noticed this because he was very private and reserved around people he didn't know well. He recognized how I go in deep in the conversation, even when I'm meeting them for the first time. He said, "You get so personal."

He then asked, "What's going through your mind when you approach someone you don't know and start talking with them? Are you thinking, this person really needs to know me or that I really need to get to know them?" I replied, "I really want to get to know them. I feel everyone is so interesting and has something to offer and I won't know what they have to offer until I talk with them."

People generally enjoy sharing about themselves. I find it hard to resist. There's just so much I want to know. For some people, I come off as too chatty, too arrogant, too nosy, or a busy body. But for those people who appreciate my inquisitive nature and see that I'm genuine in my desire to get to know them, we become fast friends. This is why after I hike with someone for the first time, it's like we've known each other forever.

However, this creates issues for me because once I get to know someone, they always want to keep in touch. I'm always excited about this at first because we truly did have a great connection, but, invariably, I choose to not stay connected. I have done this for as long as I can remember. You cannot be close to someone unless you become vulnerable, but being vulnerable is just so damn scary. I can remember many times when someone threw something personal I shared with them back in my face. I can remember each time I was vulnerable with a person and they later used what I told them to shame me. It's so painful to be vulnerable. It's so painful to trust. Yet it's so sad to be alone.

I used to think that I wanted to live by myself, never be married, and work solo in my own business. I've always strived to be as independent as possible so that I would never have to be around other people. But I always ended up craving the connection. It's so lonely, feeling like you're out on an island by yourself, like Tom Hanks in the movie, *Cast Away*.

My closest friends have learned my limitations. I give what I can when I can. I often feel sad that I'm not more consistent. Sometimes, they might hear from me once a week for a month and then they don't hear from me again for another six months.

Setting boundaries can be difficult after being traumatized.

Some of us set such strong boundaries that we don't let anyone close. Some of us set up porous boundaries that make it likely that we'll get hurt again. It's important to have boundaries, especially when your boundaries have been violated. But it's also important to recognize when your boundaries might need to move closer to you or farther away. People whom I was supposed to trust the most hurt me in terrible ways at a young age, which makes me question everyone's motives. From the myriad of ways I've been told that I'm not good enough, I'm hesitant to trust not only others but also myself.

It has caused me to let so many people down in the past because I couldn't be there for them when they needed me. So, I created a vicious cycle which is why I don't trust myself to be a good friend. I put out an olive branch to reach out for a connection, then I recoil the moment I get scared and cut off contact. Then I feel bad for doing it. So, I reach out to reconnect but then don't maintain the connection. On top of that, I'm very delayed in responding to emails, text messages, and voicemails. While, over time, I'm improving on this pattern, it's still a process I often fall back into.

We often resist what we need the most. When I reached the deepest and darkest depths of my depression, the last thing I wanted to do was connect with another human being, but it was exactly what I needed. In my journal on May 18, 2010, I asked God for "the ability to ask for help even when I don't think I need it because I can't do it all on my own."

As Jim Rohn said, "Each of us needs all of us to succeed." Being part of a community means being a part of something larger than ourselves. It gives us a sense of belonging and enables us to share in the lives and growth of others. Community offers us a place where we can work toward a common goal, find and provide opportunity, and experience safety and security. There are several ways that you can find the right community of people for you. Go online and check out some Meetup groups based on your interest or hobbies. Another great way to find a community of people is through volunteering. Connect with an organization whose mission aligns with your personal values and ethics. This could be a political, religious, or social justice organization. Or you may want to try some group classes that could range from exercising to honing your cooking skills.

Volunteering is a great way to get out into the community. It can also be very rewarding to serve. I've experienced great pleasure in finding a multitude of ways to serve. Serving others helps me to make sense of what seems to be a very messy existence at times.

Life is about making connections. At the workshop I attended with Dr. van der Kolk, I heard him say, "We're deeply social creatures. It's why much of our brain is dedicated to it."[9]

For the longest time, my pets were my closest companions. I was fortunate to have always had animals growing up. They were my true friends. Thinking back to my childhood and the comfort our pets brought to me, it was no wonder when I found my significant other dead a week and a half before I closed on the house that we were supposed to be moving into together, I had an immense desire to get a cat. Even though my apartment didn't allow pets, I couldn't wait until I moved into the house, I needed that companionship. I could just feel myself retreating inwards and I knew that no person would be able to just be with me without judgment, without wanting to push me through my pain faster than I was ready to go.

I had a vision of the cat I wanted, a fluffy gray and white female kitten that I was going to name Sophie. I have no idea where this specific vision and name came from, but I was set on it. My mother drove me around to different shelters to find "Sophie." After going to a few shelters with no success, my mom encouraged me to ease up on some of the requirements for my new cat. But at the very next shelter, the Universe opened up to me, and I saw the kitten I was looking for, a fluffy gray and white female kitten. Her name was Kina, but I renamed her Sophie. I knew six months after I got her that she deserved to have someone she could connect with too besides just me for the times I wasn't around. That's when I got Molly. They follow me everywhere and have been like my children for over 12 years.

## Activity

This is your opportunity to find "your people." This may also be the group you connect with as part of the other activities I've already mentioned in this book (e.g., a hiking, art, or exercise group). It doesn't need to be a group where you're going to spew out all your thoughts and feelings on the first encounter. It can be a group of like-minded people coming together to participate in an activity that brings enjoyment. As you participate in the activity and you get to know them, you might start to open up about difficult days you're having in the group. Or better yet, you may find a specific person in the group you connect with and open up to them.

The clocks changed back an hour on the last day of "The Body Keeps the Score" workshop at Kripalu. A confused and disheveled young woman came into the bathroom that morning. With a bright red face she asked, "Can someone please tell me what time it is? I don't know if it's 5:21 or 6:21." We told her that it was 6:21, and she went into a bathroom stall. When she came out, the redness had disappeared from her face. She thanked us for helping her. I said, "Don't worry, we got you." She started to turn away to go toward the door, but stopped, turned back, and said, "Thank you." Isn't that what we're all looking for, to have someone who will be there when we need a friend, a hug, advice, or someone just to tell us the time?

Trauma affects how we interact with others. We need to find ways that we can interact with others that won't lead us to feeling further isolated.

When I would be feeling better, I would want to connect with people, but then people weren't there for me. How could I expect that when I wasn't there for them? I have created a series of one-sided friendships where I feel I only take and give nothing in return. I'm present when I want to be present. If they happen to need me when I'm available, I do my very best to accommodate. But I bury myself in so much work that I don't have the time or energy to commit to building and sustaining friendships. It's a vicious cycle. One of my goals for 2020 was to enrich my current relationships and I'm happy to report that I achieved that goal with resounding success.

As Malcolm Gladwell says in his book, *Talking to Strangers*, "If you don't begin in a state of trust, you can't have meaningful social encounters."[13] I've had to learn over time that to have people be there for me when I need them, I need to trust people enough to get close to them to develop meaningful relationships.

I never made note of the date that I wrote this poem, but it would have been when I was a teenager. It perfectly sums up how I have felt for most of my life about preventing people from getting too close. It's called "Too Close."

Don't get too close,

For I might push you away.

Don't get too close,

For I need my space.

Don't get too close.

Give me a chance to breathe.

Don't get too close,

For you may get left far behind.

Don't get too close.

I just need a little time.

Please, don't get too close.

Trusting people has always been so difficult for me. As I read through old letters and poems about old boyfriends, I found myself regularly apologizing for how difficult my inability to trust must be for them. I would ask them to please be patient with me.

When you're trying to maintain connections or reconnect after experiencing trauma, it's important to have open lines of communication with the people you're close to. What do you need? I have to tell people right up front to expect that I won't respond right away, that I do it to everyone. I'm working on it, but it's something I have trouble with in all aspects of my life.

During my 200-hour yoga teacher training two young women became fast friends. Over the course of the training, they developed a beautiful relationship. It was wonderful for me to watch. I was also able to watch a mother and daughter interact together during the training. Both sets of women embraced each other lovingly throughout the training. Sometimes, one would way lay back on the other, just hug one another, or one would play with the other's hair.

It touched me to see these two young women build such a bond, such a love for each other, that they would embrace each other and hug each other like they were sisters or had been best friends for their entire life but, in reality, had only known each other for a short time. It was also beautiful to watch the mother and daughter interact in the same way. I had to really think and reflect on why these interactions touched me in the way they did. Part of it is because I have never had a relationship like that. I have people who love me, but I've never allowed myself to get close enough where I would allow a person to embrace me in a prolonged, loving way. I realized you can only have relationships like that when you're truly vulnerable with another individual, really let your guard down, and fully trust.

It's still hard for me, even though I have improved over time. I've tried to work on not hugging superficially, but I can tell I still typically put up an invisible wall. But maybe it's not invisible. Maybe that's why hugs aren't reciprocated in a very intimate manner like I was seeing with these women because I don't give enough of myself to them. Why are they going to be vulnerable and close to me, if they're not feeling that level of comfort from me?

Dr. Brené Brown hit the nail on the head in *Rising Strong* when she said, "Of all the things trauma takes away from us, the worst is our willingness, or even our ability, to be vulnerable. There's a reclaiming that has to happen."[14] It's why we're more likely to retreat away from the world after trauma out of fear of being hurt. It's why we're more likely not to trust ourselves, others, and new situations. But the willingness to be vulnerable will swing open the doors to healing. Your willingness to acknowledge and say that you're in pain and scared but lean into a person or experience anyways will be transformative.

Yes, the more you lean into life, the more likely you'll get hurt, but the more beauty you're likely to experience as well. It takes strength and courage to do something even though you're scared, but the moment you do, you'll realize if you can do that and everything was okay, then you can go do something that pushes you a little bit more. I've approached pushing out of the boundaries of my comfort zone as a challenge. The more I do it and succeed, the stronger and more courageous I become. It's why I feel I can accomplish anything I set my mind to. I have continued to prove it to myself repeatedly since my traumas, and so can you. Push a little further, achieve a little more, and your life will become increasingly enriched with each incremental expansion of your comfort zone.

# Chapter 10

# The Power of Routines

It takes practice to change habits and behaviors. Meditating and exercising regularly can be challenging if it's different from what you've always done. You may not be sure where it even fits in your day. Just start small. Put it in where it seems to fit best and then, over time, adjust the time of the day as you see what works and what doesn't. Maybe you start with meditating each morning but then find it difficult with distractions in your home. Maybe your children need to get ready for school and you can't steal away some time for yourself. In that case, you can move your meditation to earlier or later in the day. You can even meditate in your car before you go into work or in your house after work. If you're finding difficulty fitting self-care activities into your day, I encourage you to look for non-traditional times and locations. This includes exercise.

Consider exercising during your lunch break. Or if you find that exercising after work is challenging because you're so exhausted you can't even muster up any additional energy to do anything else, then move your exercise to first thing in the morning. What you may actually find is that you have more energy to approach work if you begin your day with exercise. You'll likely be more productive and won't be as tired by the end of the day. Explore your options of where to place different activities during your day. Find what location works best and then you can formulate a daily routine around the time that these activities fit best.

You want to incorporate a minimum of one self-care activity into every single day. You don't want it to be sporadic. Every day there should be something that you do that involves taking care of yourself and your overall well-being, whether it's exercise, meditation, journaling, or some form of creative expression.

It doesn't have to be the same self-care activity each day, but there has to be something each day. Otherwise, everyone else's priorities will begin to supersede your own. Maybe every Tuesday, Thursday, and Saturday you do some form of exercise that gets your heart rate up. Every Friday, you're going to work on a painting or another type of creative activity. Every Sunday could be time with friends or family. Try giving special names to your self-care activities if you alternate days like Meditation Monday or Sunday Solitude. Some activities are better to be included daily, but play around with your schedule and what activities serve you the most and create a self-care schedule that doesn't overwhelm you but reenergizes you.

Routines have been very important to me throughout my healing journey. Routines have given me something to focus on when my mind wants to wander into the deep hole inside me where my traumas lie. Routines have been important for me to make sure I'm including some amount of self-care into each day. Admittedly, they do create some rigidity in my life. It's hard for me to be flexible when I have much of each day planned out. Yet, it allows me to be extremely productive each day.

A morning routine I had for few years before it morphed into a variation that worked better with my current schedule was completing the Miracle Morning Life SAVERS. More detail on the Life SAVERS can be found in Hal Elrod's book, *The Miracle Morning: The Not-So-Obvious Secret Guaranteed to Transform Your Life (Before 8AM)*. As a summary, the Life SAVERS involves spending at least one minute each morning on each of the following activities:

S - Silence (e.g., meditation)

A - Affirmations

V - Visualization

E - Exercise

R - Reading

S - Scribe (e.g., journal)[15]

I still do most of these activities daily; I just spread them out throughout the day. But this routine was very important to me, and I credit it with getting me into the habit of practicing daily self-care.

When I was doing all components of The Miracle Morning in one sitting, I would spend 40-45 minutes on it. I would spend 20-25 minutes on mornings when I was more strapped for time, and 6-7 minutes when I was super strapped for time. Surprisingly, I found I could benefit from the routine even when I spent only one minute on each activity. It was amazing to see how just one minute of self-care could completely change my state and frame of mind.

When I told people that I do all these activities every single morning, they were shocked. They automatically assumed I was spending two hours of my morning doing this and that I had to get up super early. But neither were true. It takes very little time to change your frame of mind. Just deep breathing for one minute can completely change your physiology. Your heart rate will come down, your respiratory rate will decrease, and you'll feel a greater sense of calm.

The same thing goes with reading. You don't have to read for 10, 15, 20, 30, or 60 minutes at a clip to get benefits from it. I can read one section of a book each morning that takes me two to five minutes and still get a lot of benefit from it.

My daily routine now includes meditation, a sequence of restorative yoga poses, and stretches that target muscle imbalances caused by me sitting for long periods during the day, as well as listening to personal and professional development audio. I now do most of these activities at night before I go to bed, so I'm relaxed before I fall asleep.

The beginning portion of each of my meditations includes saying what I'm grateful for that day. When I think of all the little moments that are so easy to take for granted, I can't help but think about what Dr. Brené Brown said in *The Power of Vulnerability*, "If we want more joy in our lives, we have to practice gratitude."[16] In this same audiobook, she went on to describe interviews she conducted with people who have experienced horrific traumas. She said that after the trauma, when they reflected back, she repeatedly heard, "It's not that I miss the extraordinary moments that were not going to happen now that I've had this loss. What I really grieve for the most are the ordinary moments that I never paid attention to when they were here."[16] We have so much to be grateful for every day. But it's hard to see that if we remain focused on what's wrong with our lives, what we've lost, or what we don't yet have.

I've found I'm grateful for not only the small things in my life that bring me joy, but also to see others experiencing joy. I like to go on a daily walk at work. On one fall day, I was finishing my walk by strolling through the small park near my office building. I saw a large black woman, with humble means, with what seemed to be all her belongings in a small wheeling suitcase. She had a black, old-style flip phone. She was pointing it up to the sky, smiling. I kept looking up as I walked toward her, trying to see what she was looking at. She was on the sidewalk I was walking on. When I got close, she kept her arm and phone up in the air, while looking down to me, smiling, and said, "I'm talking to God." I smiled and said, "That's great!" She was so happy. I continued to smile throughout the day and for many days afterwards when I thought about the joy on her face. I still smile every time I think of her. I'm still grateful to this day to be able to take such joy while in the presence of someone else experiencing bountiful joy.

When I think of all the little moments that are so easy to take for granted, I can't help but think about how in his book, *The Untethered Soul*, Michael Singer refers to death as being our greatest teacher.

Let's say…the Angel of Death comes to you and says, "Come, it's time to go." You say, "But no. You're supposed to give me a warning so I can decide what I want to do with my last week…" Do you know what Death will say…? He'll say, "…I gave you fifty-two weeks this past year alone…Why would you need one more? What did you do

with all those?" If asked that, what are you going to say? ...
"I wasn't paying attention . . . I didn't think it mattered."
That's a pretty amazing thing to say about your life.[17]

All we ever have is this one moment. Paying attention to each
moment as if it were our last can completely transform the way we
experience life.

Conclusion

# Be Kind to Yourself

As I'm sure you already know, the healing journey is a slow-going process. Trauma can not only damage your connections to yourself and those around you, but it can change the way you see the world. As you heal, you'll have both good and bad days. I've made enormous progress since the days when I would debate on how to take my own life, but I still have days when I feel quite down. Bad days continue even as I write this book, as evidenced by this very brief journal entry a few months ago: "I feel invisible. Like I don't matter. I'm an insignificant blip." The day before, I had gone parasailing, went hiking with my sister, Nicole, and cousin, Owen, and had a wonderful time with my family. Sometimes, I still feel like I'm on a rollercoaster ride of emotions. I may snap at people, let my ego get in the way, and generally let the part of me that's still in pain get the better of me.

I also believe that life isn't going to be rainbows and unicorns every day. Life can be so hard, even if you don't experience trauma in your life. Dealing with people who have their own internal wars going on inside of them can be a struggle. At my worst, I considered wins in my day when I brushed my teeth or when I didn't sleep with yet another strange man. I'm thankful for how far I've come since those days. But I still struggle. Just like I must remind myself regularly, "Please be kind to *yourself*." Emotions come and go, and it's important that you understand bad days happen and will continue to happen even when you've made significant healing progress. They happen for everyone!

When I first started my 200-hour yoga teacher training, I began to feel very insecure about how much more work I had to do on myself. I started to identify all the areas of my life where I still needed to improve. I got really down. Sometimes, I feel like I have so far to go to overcome my traumas. Your life can change in the blink of an eye, yet it can take a lifetime just trying to get some semblance of your previous life back. I must remind myself that all I have to do is take one step at a time. It's the same way with goal setting. Many people get so overwhelmed by how far away their goal seems that they give up. That's why we previously went over the importance of chunking your goals down. Break them apart, bit by bit.

Also, remember that when aiming for any goal, although you always want to keep in mind the target you're aiming for, you don't want to miss out on all the beauty. Don't let the beauty pass you by along the way. I fell into this trap when I was pursuing the big mountains. I started to go faster, carrying heavier packs, and taking fewer breaks. Then I began to hate the journey. Love the journey so that reaching the goal will be like the cherry on top of the sundae. If you aim to make your days full of laughter, community, and healthy living, you'll learn to love your life one day at a time.

For years, I felt like I was trapped in an invisible cage that was impossible to break out of. But through many trials, tribulations, and failures, I learned how to successfully escape. We can't change everything in our life all at once. But we can make small shifts in our life that can add up to have huge effects.

Whenever I look around at my peers at workshops, my colleagues at work, or my students in the classroom, I can't help but see each of us doing the best we can. We have all experienced pain and are doing our best to muddle through a swamp of difficult thoughts, feelings, and emotions. It's unbelievable what humans are capable of overcoming. There's hope. Please know that regardless of what you've experienced, the pain will end.

Not everyone will respond to meditation, yoga, drawing, and journaling the same way. Nor will everyone respond to various healing techniques the same throughout their life. What might work for one stage of your life might not be as effective at later stages. As you progress and grow, you'll likely be ready to chart new territory in your healing journey. That's why it's good to review a host of resources from time-to-time when you're in need of something new to try.

I love kintsugi, the Japanese art of repairing broken pottery with a precious metal. Imagine how our lives would change if we viewed our pain and trauma as something beautiful. Not something to be hidden and ashamed of, but something to be highlighted in gold, silver, or platinum. Our stories make us unique. Just like pieces of pottery will break differently when they fall, so will we. When we seal our ragged edges back together with love, we come back together differently, more unique, and often more beautiful than before.

Disaster, death, and sadness will visit us all. When it comes knocking at your door, it's helpful to know you're not alone in your suffering. That's why it's important for us all to share our stories. Our stories of sadness make us feel we're not alone. Our stories of victory give us hope that the suffering will end.

Dr. Brené Brown said in *The Power of Vulnerability*, "When you own your story, here's the power of that, you get to write the ending...So when you say, 'Yes, this happened to me, but I own this story and here's how this story is going to end,' you become not the subject of the story, but you're the narrator of the story."[16] So my story is: I have been sexually violated multiple times by several different men. When I thought I was unlovable, I found a man who loved me in ways I never imagined, and then I found him dead. But my story also includes adventures around the world, me completing my PhD, and changing the lives of more students than I can count. I have a sense of empathy and compassion that makes me connect with others on a deep level. My life has been blessed in more ways than I could have ever imagined. My traumas weren't the end of my life or story; they marked the beginning of a tumultuous, but beautiful journey. There truly is beauty in darkness.

Sometimes, your traumas can help you to do amazing things. Healing can be transformative, and it's why I believe that Wolff's Law of bone is analogous to our lives. Wolff's Law states that bone will grow stronger based on the stress placed on it. Likewise, it will weaken as less stress is placed on it. The same applies to us. My trauma didn't destroy me. And yours won't destroy you either. In fact, something can come from it. Although I still have my insecurities since my traumas, my confidence has grown tremendously. From all that I've endured, I truly believe I'm unstoppable and can accomplish anything I set my mind to. I love more deeply than I ever have. I see beauty all around me. I'm grateful for every day I'm alive.

Part of what makes the effects of trauma linger for so long is when people are trying to hold on to the person and life they had before their trauma. They want so much for life to be the way it was. But true growth always requires transformation. A tree cannot become a tree without the seed transforming into something it never was before. The serotinous cones that I named my business Serotinous Life after can only open their seeds when exposed to extreme conditions, like fire. Just as the seed transforms into a tree after exposure to extreme heat, you'll transform into a better self after healing from your trauma. I encourage you to check out my list of favorite books, videos, and articles on healing from trauma and coping with life's daily stressors on my website, serotinouslife.com.

The caterpillar can never become a butterfly without transforming into something that never existed before and it requires struggling through a small opening in the cocoon. Transformation occurs slowly and often painfully, but you can make it through this journey. If either the seed or caterpillar try to hold onto what was, they'll never be able to experience the true beauty they were destined for. I believe the same holds true for us. I've used my traumas to reinvent myself. Yes, my life is different, but it's better. I'm grateful every day for all that I've been blessed with, my home, my financial security, my family and friends, health, and adventures. My life just gets better each year that I'm alive. I no longer want to go back to who I was because I'm so much better off today than I ever have been. Stop resisting the change and embrace it. There's a beautiful road ahead.

# Acknowledgments

I'm eternally grateful for the love and support of my family and friends; through them, I had the strength and courage to rise far beyond my traumas. There are no words to express the level of gratitude I feel for my mother, Laura Lacey Curler, whose unconditional love saved me in more ways than she will ever know. I know that parts of this book will be difficult for her to read. But I know she was always doing the best she could, given the circumstances. I don't hold any grudges against her and appreciate she has always encouraged the dreamer in me.

This book has been a dream of mine for many years. I'm grateful to Vikrant Shaurya and his team for helping me to finally get it published. A special thank you to Brooke Pillifant for helping me find the words to allow my thoughts to flow better through the pages, and to Wayne Purdin for his ability to polish my message with his keen attention to detail. Together, the entire team made my dream a reality. From the bottom of my heart, thank you.

I'm also grateful for the work of Dr. Brené Brown. Through the guidance of her books, I've been able to work through some of my deep-rooted shame and learned to embrace vulnerability in myself and others. I'm thankful to trauma researchers like Dr. Bessel van der Kolk, Dr. Peter A. Levine, and Dr. James S. Gordon who spent years of their life studying the effects of trauma and how to help people to move through their pain. I want to extend a special thank you to Dr. Gordon for allowing me to use his drawing exercise from his book, *The Transformation: Discovering Wholeness and Healing After Trauma*.

For anyone who feels life is swallowing you whole and you have no way to escape, please don't give up. As hard as your days may be, just hold onto to the belief, the hope that tomorrow can be better than today because it can. Day always follows night.

Warm hugs and lots of love to all,
Stephanie

# End Notes

1. Gordon, J. S. (2019, December 6-8). *Healing life's inevitable traumas* [Workshop]. Kripalu Center for Yoga & Health, Stockbridge, MA, United States.

2. Morris, T. (2014). *The seven greatest success ideas: 'A-HAs' that are guaranteed to take your life to the next level* [Audiobook]. Nightingale Conant. ASIN: B00OH76WRW.

3. Business & Self Development Resources. (2017, June 21). *How to take charge of your life - Jim Rohn personal development* [Video]. YouTube. https://youtu.be/DGIjuVbGP_A

4. Hansen, M. V. (2021, March 21). *About MVH.* http://markvictorhansen.com/about-mvh/

5. Esrick, M. (Director). (2019). *Cracked up: The Darrell Hammond story* [Film]. Healing from Trauma Film and Artemis Rising Foundation.

6. Albert, L. (2017). *Yoga for pain relief: A new approach to an ancient practice.* Dudley Court Press. ISBN-13: 978-1940013329.

7. Ensler, E. (2019, September 12). *The apology* [Book reading]. Spoken Interludes, Hastings on Hudson, NY, United States.

8. Chödrön, P. (2017). *The places that scare you: A guide to fearlessness in difficult times* [Audiobook]. Random House Audio. ASIN: B077VVGN82.

9. van der Kolk, B. (2019, November 1-3). *The body keeps the score: Brain, mind, and body in the healing of trauma* [Workshop]. Kripalu Center for Yoga & Health, Stockbridge, MA, United States.

10. Gordon, J. S. (2019). *The transformation: Discovering wholeness and healing after trauma.* HarperOne. ISBN-13: 978-0062870711.

11. Easwaran, E. (2017). *Essence of the Upanishads: A key to Indian spirituality* [Audiobook]. Blue Mountain Center of Meditation. ASIN: B0718ZZ2HZ.

12. Levine, P. A. & Frederick, A. (2016). *Waking the tiger: Healing trauma* [Audiobook]. Tantor Audio. ASIN: B01LZKDSNZ.

13. Gladwell, M. (2019). *Talking to strangers: What we should know about the people we don't know* [Audiobook]. Hachette Audio. ASIN: B07NJCG1XS.

14. Brown, B. (2015). *Rising strong: How the ability to reset transforms the way we live, love, parent, and lead* [Audiobook]. Random House Audio. ASIN: B00VSDAVI4.

15. Elrod, H. (2012). *The miracle morning: The not-so-obvious secret guaranteed to transform your life - before 8am* [Audiobook]. ASIN: B00CLMX0D4.

16. Brown, B. (2013). *The power of vulnerability: Teachings of authenticity, connection, and courage* [Audiobook]. Sounds True. ASIN: B00D1Z9RFU.

17. Singer, M. (2011). *The untethered soul: The journey beyond yourself* [Audiobook]. Tantor Audio. ASIN: B006KZ8EBQ.

Made in the USA
Las Vegas, NV
03 July 2022

51058335R00090